summer

D1257859

VEG ETA BLES

FIRST

120 VIBRANT
VEGETABLE-FORWARD RECIPES

RICARDO

Library and Archives Canada Cataloguing in Publication is available upon request.
ISBN: 978-0-525-61045-8
eBook ISBN: 978-0-525-61046-5

THE RICARDO TEAM
Author: Ricardo
Recipe Development: Lisa Birri, Nicolas Cadrin, Kareen Grondin, Michelle Marek, and Étienne Marquis
Recipe Testers: Danielle Bessette
Creative Director: Patrice Martel
Art Director: Cristine Berthiaume
Designer: Geneviève Larocque
Production Director: Paule Milette
Production Coordinator: Vanessa Risch
Graphic Artist: Linda Gravel
Photo Retouching: Jean-Michel Poirier
Photographer: David De Stefano (except the photo of Ricardo in a field: Dominique Lafond)
Assistant Photographers: Audrey Boivin, Alma Kismic, and Audrey McMahon
Food Stylists: Étienne Marquis, assisted by Stéphanie Tremblay
Accessories Stylist: Caroline Nault
Illustrator: Nadine Poirier
Multiplatform Editor in Chief: Laura Osborne
Editors: Carolyne Ann Boileau, Sarah Musgrave, Étienne Marcoux, and Pascal Henrard
Translation: Michelle Marek and Sarah Musgrave

President and Editorial Director: Brigitte Coutu
Communications and Marketing Director: Nathalie Carbonneau
Marketing Project Manager: Julie Beauchemin

ricardocuisine.com

Printed and bound in China

Published in Canada by Appetite by Random House®,
a division of Penguin Random House Canada Limited.

www.penguinrandomhouse.ca

10 9 8 7 6 5 4

Back to My Roots

My grandmother's garden has always played a big role in my life. Even now, the thought of it nourishes me. Season after season, she taught me how to seed, transplant, weed, water, and tend to the vegetable patch and six rows of raspberry bushes. I loved sitting side by side with her on her porch steps in Marieville, Quebec, eating slices of cucumber sprinkled with a little coarse salt, fresh tomato sandwiches, and yellow wax beans dripping with butter.

As soon as my parents got a house of their own, they planted their own vegetable garden. I remember coming home from summer holidays in late July and being amazed to find that, within just a few weeks, our backyard had literally exploded with life. It was the peak of the growing season, and the neighbours competed to see who had the biggest backyard bounty and who could make the best salads in the world.

And then, one day, it was my turn. My wife, Brigitte, and I planted our first plot and harvested our first tomatoes. We were tenants at the time, but our landlord loaned us some land that we made our own. Since then, our garden has grown a lot—along with our children, our happiness, and also our family business.

Even at the end of her life, when she was very ill, my mother continued to nurture our family garden and, by extension, to nurture us. After she passed away, the grief struck me hardest when I was on my knees in the yard, with my hands deep in the soil.

Throughout my career of promoting the importance of cooking together and eating together, the taste of those first summer vegetables and the joy of planting and harvesting food for the table have inspired me. My television and magazine work has evolved into a brand built on a modern vision for the art of family living. So, when we set up our new office headquarters, flagship boutique, and café on Montreal's South Shore, I made sure the roof was reinforced so that it could support a thriving garden of eighty planters and two beehives. I enjoy seeing the plants grow, be shared among colleagues and used in our test kitchen.

For me, the power of vegetables is linked with memories and family stories. And that's what I want to share with you: how fantastic vegetables can taste and how they can connect us to our roots. Finding it tough to get your kids to eat cauliflower or peas? It happens to the best of us. The important thing is to plant a seed for the future, by serving vegetables in smart, well-prepared dishes. Some life lessons take time, but in the end, we reap what we sow.

Like a vegetable garden, I hope this book becomes part of your daily life and grows with you and your family as you create your own memories.

120 Recipes That

This isn't a vegetarian cookbook. It's about vegetables playing the lead role. You'll find meat and seafood in these pages, and recipes calling for chicken stock or bacon garnish, but for a change animal proteins are really just the supporting players.

Put Vegetables First

I wanted to do things a little differently with this book. The 120 original, bright, and easy-to-make recipes—all triple-tested by our test kitchen—aren't presented according to courses, themes, chapters, or types of vegetable. Instead, they go from simple to more complex. We start off with just a few ingredients and steps, move on to preparations that are a little more involved, and then to elaborate dishes that are ideal for entertaining. The final pages show you ways to make the most of plentiful produce all year round.

The recipes cover a wide range of vegetables. Some are easy to love at first bite, while others can be a little more challenging—maybe that's eggplant, kohlrabi, endives, parsnips, or celeriac, depending on your tastes and cultural references. But they're all worth celebrating with our celery fizz cocktail!

From cover to cover, I wanted to showcase simply cooked vegetables, to highlight their vibrant textures, colours, and shapes. And, thanks to my team (kitchen, photography, styling, and artistic direction), they pop off every page. In recipe after recipe, you'll discover that eating more vegetables just means more of a good thing—and you can never get enough of a good thing.

Roasted Radish Salad (p. 68)

MY DAILY VEG

The year I was born. Montreal's Expo 67 is in full swing, and I am discovering purées. I immediatly demonstrate a talent for chewing.

1967

Boiled veg, in shades of beige or grey. Mushy, bland, and not my thing. What's more, my mother tries to cook them in her newfangled gadget: **1980** the microwave.

2019

Raw, fried, blanched, smoked, grilled, and spiralized. Vegetables are taking up more than half of my plate, and I'm preparing and presenting them in every way imaginable. Often in bowls, one of my daughters' favourite ways to eat.

2037

What role will vegetables play in the future? Meat prices are skyrocketing, and we're becoming more conscious of the environment. Will putting more veg on our plates be the solution? Either way, I'm spending more time gardening.

MAKING THE CUT

Need to turn those carrots into matchsticks or that eggplant into cubes? Cutting vegetables to the right size and shape really factors into the success of a recipe, because it affects the cooking time, the presentation, and the final taste of a dish. That holds true for everything from garlic and onion to cabbage and cucumber. The more finely sliced or grated, the more the flavour will come through. There's no arguing with science. So before getting down to work, equip yourself with two kitchen essentials: a well-sharpened knife and a quality cutting board. Your vegetables will thank you.

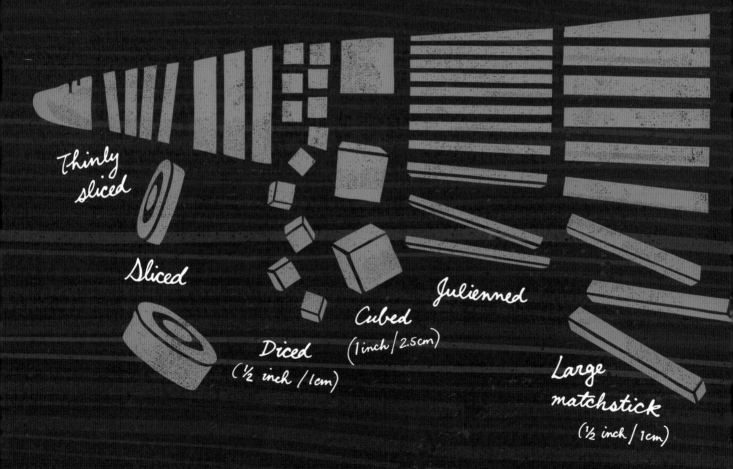

Thinly sliced

Sliced

Diced
(½ inch / 1cm)

Cubed
(1 inch / 2.5cm)

Julienned

Large matchstick
(½ inch / 1cm)

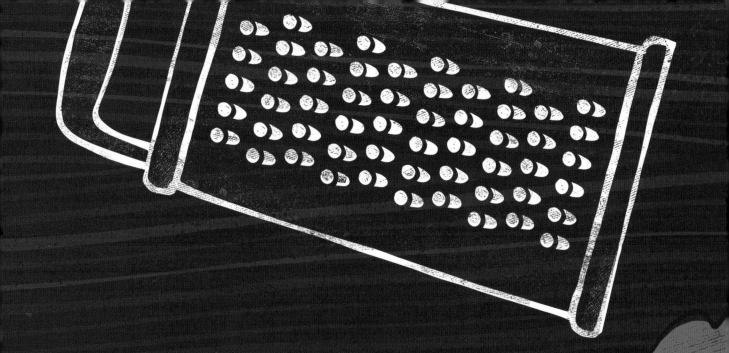

Spiralized

Grated

ROASTED TOMATOES IN OIL AND BALSAMIC VINEGAR

3 cups	(380 g) cherry tomatoes on the vine
2	garlic cloves, peeled
1/2 cup	(125 ml) olive oil
2 tbsp	(30 ml) balsamic vinegar
6 to 8	slices of crusty bread or focaccia

With the rack in the middle position, preheat the oven to 400°F (200°C).

In a glass or ceramic baking dish, drizzle the tomatoes and garlic with 2 tbsp (30 ml) of the olive oil. Season generously with salt and pepper. Bake for 20 minutes or until the tomatoes are tender and have burst slightly. Remove from the oven.

Transfer to a serving platter. Add the remaining oil and drizzle with the vinegar.

Serve the tomatoes as an appetizer with bread for dipping in the oil and vinegar dressing.

NOTE *This is our version of the classic olive oil and balsamic vinegar combo.*

PREPARATION	COOKING	SERVINGS	FREEZES
15 MIN	20 MIN	4 APPETIZERS	–

ZUCCHINI WITH PARMESAN

1 cup	(70 g) freshly grated Parmesan cheese
1/4 cup	(60 ml) vegetable oil
2 tsp	dried oregano
1/2 tsp	crushed red pepper flakes
3	zucchini, cut lengthwise into wedges

With the rack in the middle position, preheat the oven to broil.

In a large bowl, combine the Parmesan, oil, oregano, and red pepper flakes. Add the zucchini wedges and toss to coat with the cheese mixture.

On a non-stick baking sheet or a sheet lined with aluminum foil, place the zucchini wedges skin-side down. Season with salt and pepper.

Bake for 8 minutes or until golden brown.

Serve the zucchini with a grilled flank steak or chicken cutlets.

PREPARATION	COOKING	SERVINGS	FREEZES
15 MIN	8 MIN	4	–

EDAMAME BAR SNACKS

1	bag (17 oz/500 g) frozen whole edamame

LIME AND CHILI

1 1/2 tsp	fleur de sel
1 tsp	chili powder
1	lime, zest finely grated

SPICY SESAME SALT

2 tsp	sesame salt
1 tsp	fleur de sel
1/8 tsp	crushed red pepper flakes

SALT AND VINEGAR

1 tbsp	(15 ml) sherry vinegar (or your preferred vinegar)
1 1/2 tsp	fleur de sel

In a pot of boiling salted water, cook the edamame for 3 minutes. Drain. Pat dry and place in a large bowl.

Add the seasoning salt of your choice and toss to coat the beans. Serve immediately.

NOTE *Whole soybeans (edamame) are easily shelled by pressing on the shell with your teeth and sliding the beans out.*

PREPARATION	COOKING	SERVINGS	FREEZES
5 MIN	5 MIN	6	–

Chili and Lime Salt

DIPPING IN
A NEW SPIN ON THE VEGGIE PLATTER

AN EYE-CATCHING ASSORTMENT OF VEGETABLES (HELLO, FENNEL, RAINBOW CARROTS, AND RED ENDIVES!). DIPS REINVENTED WITH INTERNATIONAL SEASONINGS AND ALTERNATIVE BASES (GOODBYE, MAYO!). THE UPDATED CRUDITÉ PLATTER FEELS 100% FRESH AND NEW.

Aïoli

Broccoli Pesto (p. 75)

Carrot and Cashew Dip

Sesame Salt

Pistachio Dukka

Beet Hummus

21

CHILI AND LIME SALT

2 tbsp	fleur de sel
2 tbsp	chili powder
1 tsp	harissa powder
1/2	lime, zest finely grated

In a bowl, combine all of the ingredients.

Serve with crudités or on hard-boiled eggs, or use to season salads. The chili and lime salt will keep for 1 month in an airtight container at room temperature.

NOTE *You can find harissa powder at most grocery stores. You can also substitute 1/4 tsp cayenne pepper.*

PREPARATION 5 MIN	**MAKES** 1/4 CUP (60 ML)
COOKING –	**FREEZES** –

SESAME SALT

1/4 cup	(35 g) black sesame seeds
1 tsp	fleur de sel

In a skillet over medium heat, toast the sesame seeds for 5 minutes or until they are fragrant. Place in a bowl and let cool.

Using a spice mill or mortar and pestle, grind the sesame seeds. Add the salt.

Serve with crudités or hard-boiled eggs, or on rice. The sesame salt will keep for 1 month in an airtight container at room temperature.

PREPARATION 2 MIN	**MAKES** 1/4 CUP (60 ML)
COOKING 5 MIN	**FREEZES** –

AÏOLI

1	egg yolk
1 tbsp	(15 ml) lemon juice
2 tsp	(10 ml) Dijon mustard
1/4 tsp	salt
1	small garlic clove, minced
1 cup	(250 ml) canola oil

In a bowl, whisk together the egg yolk, lemon juice, mustard, salt, and garlic. Add about one-third of the oil, drop by drop, whisking all the while. As soon as the mayonnaise begins to form, add the remaining oil in a steady stream, continuing to whisk. Pepper to taste.

Serve with crudités, hard-boiled eggs, or poached fish. The aïoli will keep for 5 days in an airtight container in the refrigerator.

PREPARATION	MAKES
10 MIN	1 CUP (250 ML)
COOKING	FREEZES
–	–

PISTACHIO DUKKA

3/4 cup	(100 g) shelled unsalted toasted pistachios
2 tbsp	toasted sesame seeds
1 tsp	ground turmeric
1 tsp	garlic salt
1 tsp	onion salt
1 tsp	sweet paprika
1 tsp	ground cumin
1 tsp	ground coriander
1/8 tsp	cayenne pepper
1/8 tsp	ground cardamom
1/8 tsp	ground fennel
	Olive oil, to serve
	Bread cubes, to serve

In a small food processor, or using a mortar and pestle, grind the pistachios until fine. Add the remaining ingredients. Season generously with pepper and mix well. Place in a bowl.

Pour the olive oil into another bowl. Serve with the bread cubes, dipping them first in the olive oil, then in the dukka. This is also delicious with crudités. The dukka will keep for 1 month in an airtight container at room temperature or for 3 months in the freezer.

PREPARATION	MAKES
20 MIN	1 CUP (250 ML)
COOKING	FREEZES
–	YES

CARROT AND CASHEW DIP

2	carrots, cut into small pieces
1	garlic clove, sliced
1/2 tsp	ground turmeric
1/8 tsp	ground cumin
1 tbsp	(15 ml) olive oil, plus more for serving
3/4 cup	(180 ml) water
1/4 cup	(30 g) toasted cashews
1/4 cup	(60 ml) tahini
2 tbsp	(30 ml) lemon juice

In a non-stick skillet over medium-high heat, brown the carrots, garlic, and ground spices in the oil. Add 1/2 cup (125 ml) of the water and continue cooking over medium heat for 5 minutes or until the carrots are tender and the liquid has evaporated. Season with salt and pepper. Let cool.

In a food processor, grind the cashews. Add the tahini, lemon juice, the carrot mixture, and the remaining water. Process until the mixture is smooth and homogeneous. Using a spatula, scrape down the sides of the processor bowl occasionally. Add more water, if needed. Season to taste.

Serve with crudités or crackers. Add a drizzle of olive oil and pepper, if desired. The dip will keep for 1 week in an airtight container in the refrigerator.

PREPARATION	COOKING	MAKES	FREEZES
20 MIN	15 MIN	1 1/2 CUPS (375 ML)	–

BEET HUMMUS

3/4 lb	(340 g) cooked beets, peeled and cut into pieces
1/4 cup	(60 ml) tahini
1 tsp	(5 ml) lemon juice
	Chervil leaves (optional)

In a food processor, process the beets into a smooth purée. Using a spatula, scrape down the sides of the processor bowl occasionally. Transfer to a separate bowl. Add the tahini and lemon juice. Season with salt and pepper and mix well.

Serve with crudités, fresh pita bread, or pita chips. Top with chervil leaves, if desired. The hummus will keep for 1 week in an airtight container in the refrigerator.

PREPARATION	COOKING	MAKES	FREEZES
10 MIN	–	1 1/2 CUPS (375 ML)	–

ALL-GREEN SALAD

VINAIGRETTE

3 tbsp	(45 ml) olive oil
2 tbsp	(30 ml) lemon juice
1	small garlic clove, finely chopped

SALAD

4 cups	(100 g) watercress sprouts or watercress
4 cups	(100 g) tender lettuce or Boston lettuce leaves
2 cups	(50 g) baby spinach
1	English cucumber, thinly sliced
1	green apple, deseeded, thinly sliced, and tossed with lemon juice
2 tbsp	(30 ml) toasted pumpkin seeds

VINAIGRETTE

In a bowl, combine all of the ingredients. Season with salt and pepper.

SALAD

In a salad bowl, combine the watercress, lettuce, spinach, cucumber, and apple. Just before serving, drizzle with the vinaigrette and mix well. Adjust the seasoning. Top with pumpkin seeds.

Serve as an appetizer or as a side for grilled meat, fish, or a quiche.

PREPARATION	COOKING	SERVINGS	FREEZES
15 MIN	–	4 TO 6	–

SALT-ROASTED BEETS

4 to 6	whole beets, unpeeled and washed
4 cups	(1.1 kg) coarse salt

Preheat the oven to 350°F (180°C).

Place the beets in an 8-inch (20 cm) square glass or ceramic baking dish. Cover completely with the salt. Bake for 1 hour 30 minutes. Remove from the oven.

Let the beets cool in the salt before peeling them, about 2 hours. They are perfect for beet carpaccio, in salads, or with meat or poultry. The beets, once peeled, will keep for 2 weeks in an airtight container in the refrigerator.

NOTE *The salt, once dry, can be kept in an airtight container and reused to cook beets.*

PREPARATION 10 MIN	**MAKES** 4 TO 6
COOKING 1 H 30	**FREEZES** –
COOLING 2 H	

BEET CARPACCIO

2	salt-roasted beets, peeled
1/2 cup	(125 ml) crème fraîche
2 tbsp	finely chopped dill
1/8 tsp	ground caraway seeds
	Olive oil, for serving

Finely slice the beets, ideally with a mandoline.

Place the beet slices on a plate. Garnish with crème fraîche. Sprinkle with the dill and caraway. Drizzle with a bit of olive oil and season to taste with salt and pepper.

Serve as an appetizer.

PREPARATION 10 MIN	**SERVINGS** 4
COOKING –	**FREEZES** –

SESAME CUCUMBER SALAD

2 tbsp	(30 ml) rice vinegar
2 tbsp	(30 ml) vegetable oil
1 tbsp	(15 ml) toasted sesame oil
1 tbsp	toasted sesame seeds
1 tbsp	(15 ml) honey
1 tsp	crushed red pepper flakes
2	English cucumbers

In a large bowl, whisk together all of the ingredients except the cucumbers. Season with salt and pepper.

Using a spiralizer, cut the cucumbers into ribbons. Cut the ribbons in five pieces to shorten them.

Just before serving, add the cucumbers to the vinaigrette and mix well. Serve immediately.

Delicious with tofu, grilled fish, or satay skewers.

PREPARATION	COOKING	SERVINGS	FREEZES
20 MIN	–	4 TO 6	–

BOK CHOY WITH GARLIC AND LEMON

1 1/2 lb	(675 g) baby bok choy, cut in half lengthwise
2	garlic cloves, thinly sliced
2 tbsp	(30 ml) vegetable oil
1/2 cup	(125 ml) vegetable or chicken broth
1 tbsp	(15 ml) lemon juice
1 tsp	finely grated lemon zest

In a large non-stick skillet over medium-high heat, brown the cut side of the bok choy and garlic in the oil. Season with salt and pepper. Add the broth and lemon juice.

Cover and let simmer over medium heat for 2 to 3 minutes or until the bok choy is tender. Transfer to a serving platter. Drizzle with the broth and sprinkle with the lemon zest.

Serve with roasted chicken, fish, or tofu.

PREPARATION	COOKING	SERVINGS	FREEZES
15 MIN	12 MIN	4 TO 6	–

FLAT-OUT EASY
IN PRAISE OF THE SHEET PAN

AMONG COOKING TOOLS, THE SHEET PAN TAKES THE PRIZE FOR PRACTICALITY. WE LOVE IT BECAUSE IT HELPS SAVE TIME ON WEEKNIGHTS BY COOKING EVERYTHING IN ONE SHOT. THIS SIMPLE METHOD ALSO HAS THE POWER TO TRANSFORM THE FLAVOURS OF VEGETABLES. WHEN CARROTS OR BRUSSELS SPROUTS ARE ROASTED AND GENTLY CARAMELIZED IN THE OVEN, IT'S LIKE DISCOVERING THEM ALL OVER AGAIN.

Cauliflower Popcorn

Brussels Sprout Chips

Baked Home Fries

ROASTED CARROTS

---

4 lb	**(1.8 kg) Nantes carrots, mix of colours, peeled**
2 tbsp	**(30 ml) olive oil**

With the rack in the middle position, preheat the oven to 400°F (200°C).

On a non-stick baking sheet or a sheet lined with parchment paper, combine the carrots with the oil. Season with salt and pepper.

Bake for 35 minutes or until the carrots are tender, stirring halfway through cooking.

PREPARATION	SERVINGS
10 MIN	6
COOKING	**FREEZES**
35 MIN	–

CAULIFLOWER POPCORN

1	**cauliflower, cut into small florets**
2 tbsp	**(30 ml) olive oil**

With the rack in the middle position, preheat the oven to 400°F (200°C).

On a non-stick baking sheet or a sheet lined with parchment paper, combine the cauliflower with the oil. Season with salt and pepper.

Bake for 35 minutes or until the cauliflower is tender and golden brown, stirring occasionally.

Delicious sprinkled with chili and lime salt (recipe p. 22).

PREPARATION	SERVINGS
10 MIN	4 TO 6
COOKING	**FREEZES**
35 MIN	–

BRUSSELS SPROUT CHIPS

2 lb	(900 g) Brussels sprouts
2 tbsp	(30 ml) olive oil

With the rack in the middle position, preheat the oven to 350°F (180°C).

Trim the base of the Brussels sprouts to remove the outer leaves. Cut the base again and continue removing leaves until only the heart remains. You should have about 10 cups (340 g) of Brussels sprout leaves. You can finely slice the hearts and add them to soups or salads.

On a non-stick baking sheet or a sheet lined with parchment paper, combine the leaves with the oil. Season with salt and pepper.

Bake for 20 minutes or until the leaves are lightly golden, stirring occasionally.

PREPARATION	**SERVINGS**
20 MIN	4 TO 6
COOKING	**FREEZES**
20 MIN	–

BAKED HOME FRIES

2 lb	(900 g) Russet potatoes, unpeeled and cut into long wedges 1/2-inch (1 cm) thick
2 tbsp	(30 ml) olive oil

With the rack in the middle position, preheat the oven to 400°F (200°C).

On a non-stick baking sheet or a sheet lined with parchment paper, combine the potatoes with the oil. Season with salt and pepper. Arrange the potato wedges skin-side down.

Bake for 45 minutes or until golden.

Delicious with aïoli (recipe p. 23).

PREPARATION	**SERVINGS**
15 MIN	4 TO 6
COOKING	**FREEZES**
45 MIN	–

STEAMED KOHLRABI WITH DASHI-STYLE BROTH

4	small kohlrabi with leaves
1/4 cup	(60 ml) chicken broth
2 tbsp	(30 ml) reduced-sodium soy sauce
1 tbsp	(15 ml) fish sauce
1 tbsp	(15 ml) rice vinegar
1 tbsp	(15 ml) honey
1/2 tsp	(2.5 ml) cherry or Fresno pepper, seeded and diced

Place a steamer basket in the bottom of a pot. Add water up to the base of the steamer. Cover and bring to a boil.

Remove the leaves from the kohlrabi and set aside. Peel the kohlrabi using a vegetable peeler and cut into wedges.

Place the kohlrabi in the steamer basket. Cover and steam until fork-tender, about 15 minutes, topping up the water as needed. Add the leaves and continue steaming for 5 minutes.

Meanwhile, in a small pot, bring the broth, soy sauce, fish sauce, vinegar, and honey to a boil.

Transfer the kohlrabi to bowls. Pour the broth over them and garnish with the pepper.

Serve with grilled pork or shrimp.

NOTE *We mimic dashi (dried bonito and seaweed broth) by adding fish sauce to the broth.*

PREPARATION	COOKING	SERVINGS	FREEZES
15 MIN	25 MIN	4	—

LEMON-GRILLED ARTICHOKES

4	artichokes
2	garlic cloves, unpeeled
2 tbsp	(30 ml) olive oil
1	lemon, cut in half
3/4 cup	(180 ml) mayonnaise

Place a steamer basket in the bottom of a large pot. Add water up to the base of the steamer. Cover and bring to a boil.

Remove the outer leaves from the base of the artichokes. Using a knife, cut off and discard the top third of the artichoke. Using scissors, trim the tops of the remaining leaves. Peel the stem. Cut the artichokes in half, keeping the stem. Using a spoon, remove the furry choke. Place the artichokes and garlic in the steamer. Cover and steam until the artichokes are fork-tender, about 15 minutes, topping up the water as needed. Remove the artichokes and garlic.

In a large non-stick skillet over medium-high heat, brown the artichokes in the oil with the garlic and lemon, about 5 minutes (see note).

In a small bowl, mash the garlic with a fork. Remove the peels. Add the mayonnaise and juice from the grilled lemons. Season with salt and pepper and mix well. Serve the artichokes with the mayonnaise.

Serve as an appetizer, as a tapas, or with grilled meat.

NOTE *Depending on the size of the artichokes, you can brown them in two batches or at the same time using two skillets.*

PREPARATION	COOKING	SERVINGS	FREEZES
25 MIN	20 MIN	4	–

43

SPIRALIZED ZUCCHINI FRIES

	Vegetable oil, for frying
1/2 cup	(125 ml) mayonnaise
1 tbsp	(15 ml) Sriracha sauce
2	large zucchini
2	eggs
2 tbsp	(30 ml) water
1 cup	(150 g) unbleached all-purpose flour
2 tsp	salt
1 tsp	sweet paprika
1/4 tsp	ground pepper

Preheat the oil in a deep fryer to 375°F (190°C). Line a baking sheet with paper towel.

In a small bowl, combine the mayonnaise and Sriracha. Season lightly with salt and pepper to taste. Set aside.

Using a spiralizer, cut the zucchini into ribbons, then cut the ribbons in three to shorten them.

In another bowl, using a fork, whisk the eggs with the water. In a third bowl, combine the flour, salt, paprika, and pepper. Toss half of the zucchini at a time in the egg mixture. Drain. Toss the zucchini in the flour mixture to coat. Shake to remove any excess. Set aside on a plate.

Fry one-third of the zucchini at a time for 2 to 3 minutes or until golden brown. Watch in case the oil splatters. Drain on the paper towel–lined baking sheet. Season with salt and pepper.

Serve immediately, as a bar snack, with the spicy mayonnaise.

PREPARATION	COOKING	SERVINGS	FREEZES
20 MIN	6 MIN	4	–

MAPLE-GLAZED MUSHROOMS

2 tbsp	(30 ml) vegetable oil
1 lb	(450 g) small white button mushrooms
1	garlic clove, peeled
2 tbsp	(30 ml) maple syrup
2 tbsp	(30 ml) soy sauce
1 tbsp	finely chopped chives

In a large non-stick skillet over medium heat, heat the oil. Add the mushrooms and garlic. Cook for 5 minutes, stirring. Add the maple syrup and soy sauce. Continue cooking for 5 minutes or until the mushrooms are tender and the sauce has completely evaporated. Remove the garlic. Add the chives. Season with salt and pepper.

Delicious as a tapas, or as a side dish for a pork roast or an omelette.

PREPARATION	COOKING	SERVINGS	FREEZES
5 MIN	10 MIN	4	–

LEEK SOUP

4 cups	(1 L) chicken broth
1 cup	(250 ml) buttered leeks (recipe p. 230)
2 tsp	(10 ml) Worcestershire sauce
12	slices baguette
1 cup	(100 g) grated Gruyère cheese

In a pot, bring the broth, leeks, and Worcestershire to a boil. Let simmer 15 minutes.

With the rack in the middle position, preheat the oven to broil.

Place four heat-proof soup bowls on a baking sheet. Transfer the soup into the bowls. Place two or three slices of baguette on top of each, and sprinkle with the Gruyère cheese. Bake for 5 minutes or until the cheese is melted and golden.

NOTE *For a classic French onion soup, replace the chicken broth with a beef broth and the buttered leeks with the same quantity of caramelized onions (recipe p. 238).*

PREPARATION	COOKING	SERVINGS	FREEZES
10 MIN	20 MIN	4	YES

ROASTED WHITE ASPARAGUS WITH HERBS

1 lb	(450 g) white asparagus, trimmed
1/4 cup	(60 ml) olive oil
3	sprigs rosemary
2	sprigs thyme
1	sprig sage
2	garlic cloves, cut in half
1 tbsp	(15 ml) lemon juice
1/2 cup	(125 ml) chicken broth
1 tbsp	currants
2 tbsp	freshly grated Parmesan cheese

In a large skillet over medium-high heat, sauté the asparagus in the oil with the herbs and garlic until golden. Set aside. Deglaze the pan with the lemon juice. Add the broth and currants.

Continue cooking for 5 minutes or until the broth is reduced by three-quarters. Place the asparagus back in the skillet and toss to coat with the sauce. Season with salt and pepper.

Transfer to a serving platter. Top with the roasted herbs and garlic and the Parmesan.

Delicious with lamb chops or a grilled rib steak.

PREPARATION	COOKING	SERVINGS	FREEZES
15 MIN	15 MIN	4	–

SPAGHETTI SQUASH MARINARA

1	spaghetti squash (about 2.2 lb/1 kg), unpeeled and sliced into 2-inch (5 cm) rounds, seeds removed
2 tbsp	(30 ml) olive oil
2 cups	(500 ml) tomato sauce (recipe p. 239), hot
1/4 cup	(20 g) freshly grated Parmesan cheese
	Fresh basil leaves, for serving

With the rack in the middle position, preheat the oven to 400°F (200°C). Line a baking sheet with a silicone mat or parchment paper.

Place the squash slices on the baking sheet. Drizzle with the oil and season with salt and pepper. Bake for 35 minutes or until tender.

Transfer the squash to plates. Using a fork, scrape the squash towards the centre of each slice, creating a layer of squash. Pour 1/2 cup (125 ml) of tomato sauce onto the centre of each squash slice, and then top with Parmesan and basil leaves.

Serve as an appetizer. Delicious as a side to grilled meat.

PREPARATION	COOKING	SERVINGS	FREEZES
15 MIN	35 MIN	4	–

YELLOW BEAN CACIO E PEPE

1 1/2 lb	(675 g) yellow beans, trimmed
3	egg yolks
1/2 cup	(35 g) freshly grated pecorino Romano cheese
1/2 cup	(35 g) freshly grated Parmesan cheese, plus more for serving
2 tbsp	(30 ml) butter
2 tbsp	finely chopped flat-leaf parsley
1	lemon, zest finely grated

In a pot of boiling salted water, cook the beans until they are very tender, about 10 minutes. Remove 1 1/2 cups (375 ml) of the cooking water. Drain the beans. On a work surface, split the beans in half lengthwise (optional, see note).

In a bowl, whisk together the yolks and the cheeses. Generously season with salt and pepper. Gradually add 3/4 cup (180 ml) of the cooking water, whisking all the while.

In the same pot over medium-low heat, melt the butter. Add the yolk mixture and cook, whisking constantly, until the mixture begins to thicken and becomes smooth, about 10 minutes. Add the parsley, lemon zest, and beans. Add more cooking water if needed to thin the sauce or to fix it if it has separated. Mix well to coat the beans in the sauce. Adjust the seasoning.

Top with more Parmesan and season with pepper.

Serve as an appetizer, as you would pasta *cacio e pepe*.

NOTE *Splitting the beans in half this way makes them finer, more flexible, and more able to absorb the sauce. If you leave them whole, add 2 minutes to the cooking time after you add the beans to the sauce.*

PREPARATION	COOKING	SERVINGS	FREEZES
35 MIN	20 MIN	4 TO 6	–

ROASTED LEEKS WITH ROMESCO SAUCE

ROMESCO SAUCE

2	red bell peppers, cut in half and deseeded
1	Italian tomato, cut in half
1	cherry pepper
1/4 cup	(60 ml) olive oil
1/4 cup	(40 g) toasted blanched almonds
3 tbsp	(10 g) chopped stale bread
1	garlic clove, chopped
2 tsp	(10 ml) sherry vinegar
1/4 tsp	smoked paprika
1/8 tsp	ground cumin

LEEKS

3	medium leeks, cut in half lengthwise
1/4 cup	(60 ml) olive oil

ROMESCO SAUCE

With the rack in the middle position, preheat the oven to 450°F (230°C).

On a non-stick baking sheet or a sheet lined with parchment paper, place the bell peppers (skin-side up), tomatoes, and cherry pepper. Toss with 1 tbsp (15 ml) of the oil. Bake for 25 minutes or until the peppers begin to colour. Transfer the vegetables to an airtight container and let cool for 20 minutes. Remove the skin and seeds.

In a blender, purée the peppers, tomato, and cherry pepper with the remaining ingredients. Season with salt and pepper. Set aside.

LEEKS

On the same baking sheet, place the leeks cut-side down. Drizzle with the oil. Season with salt and pepper. Cover with aluminum foil but do not seal. Bake for 20 minutes or until the leeks are tender and golden. Remove the first layer of leek if it has toughened during the baking.

Spread half the Romesco sauce over the bottom of a serving platter. Place the leeks cut-side up in the sauce. Serve with the remaining sauce on the side.

Serve as an appetizer.

NOTE *The sauce is also great with grilled asparagus, in sandwiches, or with grilled meats.*

PREPARATION	COOKING	COOLING	SERVING	FREEZES
30 MIN	45 MIN	20 MIN	6	SAUCE ONLY

JUICED UP
SAYING CHEERS TO VEGETABLES

THERE'S SOMETHING SO SATISFYING ABOUT MAKING YOUR OWN JUICE. FIRST OFF, INGREDIENTS TASTE DELICIOUS WHEN THEY'RE FRESHLY PRESSED. WHAT'S MORE, JUICING IS A GREAT WAY TO EMPTY THE REFRIGERATOR, AND USE UP WHATEVER VEGGIES YOU HAPPEN TO HAVE ON HAND. ADDING A BIT OF FRUIT SWEETENS THE DEAL AND GIVES AN ENDLESS ARRAY OF OPTIONS.

Tomato Juice

Carrot and Strawberry Juice

**Carrot, Bell Pepper,
and Orange Juice**

Celery and Fennel Juice

CARROT AND STRAWBERRY JUICE

3	carrots, peeled
1 1/2 cups	(210 g) strawberries, trimmed

Cut the carrots into pieces, if necessary. Pass through a juicer. Pour into a glass.

NOTE *Use vegetables and fruit straight from the refrigerator for a cold juice, or serve over ice cubes.*

PREPARATION 10 MIN	**SERVINGS** 1
COOKING –	**FREEZES** –

TOMATO JUICE

1 cup	(180 g) chopped tomatoes
1/3 cup	(75 ml) water
1 tsp	(5 ml) tomato paste
1 tsp	(5 ml) lemon juice
1	pinch salt

In a pot, bring all of the ingredients to a boil and let simmer for 10 minutes. Using a small blender, blend until smooth. Pass through a sieve and let cool completely in the refrigerator. The tomato juice will keep for 1 week in an airtight container in the refrigerator. This recipe doubles easily.

PREPARATION 10 MIN	**COOLING** 1 H
COOKING 12 MIN	**SERVINGS** 1

CELERY AND FENNEL JUICE

2	celery stalks
1	kale leaf
1/2	fennel bulb
1	Cortland apple, deseeded

Cut the vegetables and apple into pieces, if necessary. Pass through a juicer. Pour into a glass.

NOTE *Use vegetables and fruit straight from the refrigerator for a cold juice, or serve over ice cubes.*

PREPARATION	SERVINGS
10 MIN	1
COOKING	**FREEZES**
–	–

CARROT, BELL PEPPER, AND ORANGE JUICE

3	carrots, peeled
1/2	bell pepper, yellow or orange, deseeded
1	orange, peeled

Cut the vegetables and orange into pieces, if necessary. Pass through a juicer. Pour into a glass.

NOTE *Use vegetables and fruit straight from the refrigerator for a cold juice, or serve over ice cubes.*

PREPARATION	SERVINGS
10 MIN	1
COOKING	**FREEZES**
–	–

FIELD TO FEAST

For me, agriculture is as fundamental to a culture as the languages we speak, the music we listen to, and the cuisines we share. It starts with respect for the earth, and for the hard work that goes into keeping it rich and fertile. Understanding what I'm eating, and recognizing the sacrifice and dedication of the producer behind it, strengthens the connection I have with food. And cooking vegetables that I've grown myself is not only gratifying, it's also a great incentive for reducing food waste. I recommend choosing varieties of vegetables that are cultivated close to home, as this has an immediate, positive, and concrete effect on regional economies. Eating local is changing our world—and our children's future—for the better.

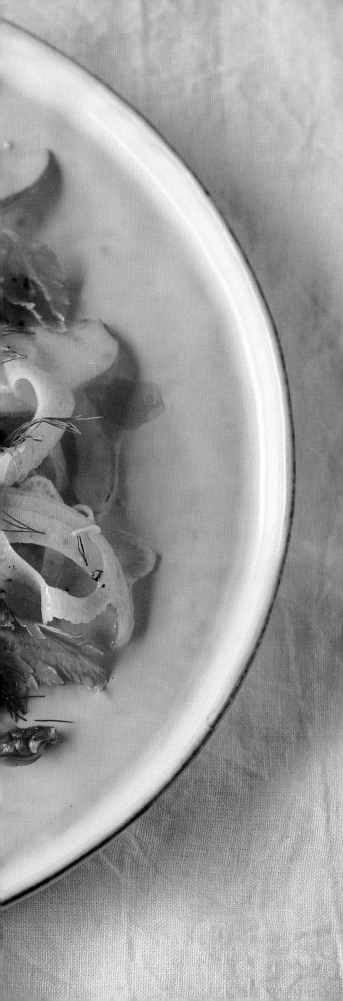

FENNEL AND CELERY SALAD

2 tbsp	(30 ml) lemon juice
2 tbsp	(30 ml) olive oil
1 tsp	(5 ml) honey
1	fennel bulb, sliced on a mandoline
1	pear, sliced and tossed in lemon juice
2	celery stalks, sliced diagonally
1/4 cup	(10 g) celery leaves
1/4 cup	(25 g) chopped toasted pecans
	Fennel fronds, for serving

In a large bowl, combine the lemon juice, oil, and honey. Season with salt and pepper. Add the fennel, pear, celery, celery leaves, and pecans. Mix to coat with the vinaigrette. Adjust the seasoning. Place the salad on plates and garnish with fennel fronds.

Serve as an appetizer.

PREPARATION	**SERVINGS**
10 MIN	4
COOKING	**FREEZES**
–	–

SALAD TOSS-UP
SO MANY WINNING COMBINATIONS

Roasted Cipollini
Salad (p. 70)

+

Potato and
Corn Salad (p. 71)

+

Roasted Radish
Salad (p. 68)

+

CREATING A STUNNING SALAD IS A SIMPLE EQUATION: TAKE A ROASTED OR FRESH VEGETABLE, ADD A BED OF LETTUCE, A SOURCE OF PROTEIN, AND A VINAIGRETTE OR SEASONED MAYO, AND THERE YOU GO! THE SPECIFICS OF THE INGREDIENTS ARE INTERCHANGEABLE, SO JUST USE THESE RECIPES AS SUGGESTIONS AND EXPERIMENT FROM THERE—IT'S JUST A MATTER OF FINDING THE COMBINATIONS YOU LIKE BEST.

ROASTED RADISH SALAD

CHIMICHURRI SAUCE

1/2 cup	(125 ml) olive oil
2 tbsp	(30 ml) red wine vinegar
1	green onion, finely chopped
1	small garlic clove, finely chopped
1/4 cup	(10 g) finely chopped flat-leaf parsley
2 tbsp	finely chopped cilantro
2 tbsp	finely chopped chives
1 tbsp	finely chopped oregano

ROASTED RADISHES

1 lb	(450 g) radishes cut in half or quarters, depending on their size
3 tbsp	(45 ml) olive oil
1 tbsp	(15 ml) honey

SALAD

6 cups	(140 g) arugula
1 cup	(120 g) crumbled feta cheese

CHIMICHURRI SAUCE

In a bowl, combine all of the ingredients. Set aside.

ROASTED RADISHES

In a large non-stick skillet over high heat, cook the radishes in the oil until tender and golden, about 10 minutes. Season with salt and pepper. Drizzle with the honey and continue cooking for 1 minute. Remove from the heat (see note).

SALAD

Place the arugula on a serving platter. Top with the radishes and feta. Drizzle with the chimichurri.

Delicious with grilled beef, white fish, or chicken.

NOTE *The roasted radishes are also a great side dish.*

PREPARATION	COOKING	SERVINGS	FREEZES
25 MIN	12 MIN	6	–

ROASTED CIPOLLINI SALAD

CREAMY ALMOND DRESSING

1/4 cup	(30 g) blanched, sliced almonds, toasted
2 tbsp	(30 ml) vegetable oil
2 tbsp	(30 ml) white wine vinegar
1 tbsp	(15 ml) honey
1 tbsp	(15 ml) water
1	small garlic clove, chopped

ROASTED CIPOLLINI

1 lb	(450 g) cipollini onions, peeled and cut in half or quarters, depending on their size
2 tbsp	(30 ml) vegetable oil

SALAD

6 cups	(140 g) baby spinach
1	can (19 oz/540 ml) chickpeas, drained and rinsed

CREAMY ALMOND DRESSING

In a small blender, purée all the ingredients until smooth and creamy. Add water to thin it out, if needed. Season with salt and pepper.

ROASTED CIPOLLINI

In a non-stick skillet over medium heat, cook the onions in the oil, stirring occasionally, until tender and golden. Season with salt and pepper. Let cool.

SALAD

Place the spinach on a large serving platter. Top with the chickpeas and onions. Drizzle with the dressing.

Great with sausages, shrimp, or chicken.

PREPARATION	COOKING	SERVINGS	FREEZES
25 MIN	20 MIN	4 TO 6	–

POTATO AND CORN SALAD

SPICY MAYONNAISE

1/4 cup	(60 ml) mayonnaise
2 tbsp	(30 ml) vegetable oil
1 tbsp	(15 ml) lemon juice
1 tsp	(5 ml) Tabasco sauce
1/2 tsp	sweet paprika

POTATOES

1 1/2 lb	(675 g) baby potatoes, cut in half
1	garlic clove, finely chopped
2 tbsp	(30 ml) vegetable oil

SALAD

4	eggs
2	ears corn, cooked and kernels taken off the cob

SPICY MAYONNAISE

In a bowl, whisk together all of the ingredients. Season with salt and pepper. Refrigerate until ready to serve.

POTATOES

With the rack in the middle position, preheat the oven to 450°F (230°C).

Place the potatoes in a pot and cover with water. Season with salt. Bring to a boil and cook for 12 minutes or until fork-tender. Drain.

Lay the potatoes on a non-stick baking sheet or a sheet lined with aluminum foil. Add the garlic and oil. Season with salt and pepper and mix well. Place the potatoes cut-side down.

Bake for 15 to 20 minutes or until golden.

SALAD

Meanwhile, in a small pot, place the eggs and cover with cold water. Bring to a boil. As soon as the water begins to boil, cover the pot and remove from the heat. Let sit for 10 minutes. Remove the eggs from the water and plunge them into an ice bath to stop the cooking. Peel the eggs. Cut into wedges.

Transfer the potatoes to a serving platter. Top with the eggs and corn. Drizzle with the spicy mayonnaise.

Great with ham or canned tuna.

PREPARATION	COOKING	SERVINGS	FREEZES
20 MIN	30 MIN	4 TO 6	–

GRILLED TOFU WITH KALE AND SWEET POTATO SALAD

SWEET POTATO
3 1/2 cups	(450 g)	peeled and grated sweet potato (1 large sweet potato)
3 tbsp	(45 ml)	olive oil
1 tsp		curry powder

GRILLED TOFU
3 tbsp	(45 ml)	olive oil, plus more for the pan
2 tbsp	(30 ml)	soy sauce
2 tbsp	(30 ml)	lemon juice
1 tbsp	(15 ml)	honey
1 lb	(450 g)	firm tofu, cut into 8 slices

SALAD
1/4 cup	(60 ml)	olive oil
1/4 cup	(60 ml)	orange juice
2 tbsp	(30 ml)	lemon juice
2 tbsp	(30 ml)	Dijon mustard
4 cups	(150 g)	finely chopped kale
4		Lebanese cucumbers, cut into half-moons
2		avocados, peeled and thinly sliced

SWEET POTATO

With the rack in the middle position, preheat the oven to 350°F (180°C). Line a baking sheet with parchment paper.

On the baking sheet, combine the sweet potato with the oil and curry powder. Season with salt and pepper. Bake for 30 minutes, without stirring, until golden. Let cool.

GRILLED TOFU

Meanwhile, combine the oil, soy sauce, lemon juice, and honey in a glass baking dish. Add the tofu and toss to coat with the marinade. Let marinate for 15 minutes at room temperature.

Heat a cast iron grill pan over high heat. Oil the pan.

Drain the tofu, reserving the marinade. Grill the tofu in the pan for 2 minutes per side. On a work surface, slice the tofu.

SALAD

In a bowl, whisk together the oil, orange juice, lemon juice, and mustard.

In another bowl, massage the kale, using your hands, to tenderize it. Add the cucumbers and sweet potato. Add half of the vinaigrette and mix well. Season with salt and pepper.

Place the salad on plates. Top with the avocado and tofu. Drizzle with the vinaigrette and the reserved marinade.

PREPARATION	MARINATING	COOKING	SERVINGS	FREEZES
30 MIN	15 MIN	35 MIN	4	–

Tuscan Kale Pesto

PESTO POWER
TAKING IT BEYOND BASIL

WHETHER IT'S USED AS A SAUCE FOR PASTA, TO DRESS POULTRY OR FISH, IN A SANDWICH, OR EVEN AS A DIP, PESTO HAS NO EQUAL. WHILE WE'LL ALWAYS LOVE THE CLASSIC BASIL VERSION, THESE BRILLIANT GREEN, VEGETABLE-FORWARD CREATIONS ARE DESTINED TO BECOME OUR NEW GO-TOS.

Artichoke Pesto

BROCCOLI PESTO

4 cups	(280 g) chopped broccoli
1/2 cup	(35 g) freshly grated Parmesan cheese
1/4 cup	(35 g) toasted pumpkin seeds
1/2 cup	(15 g) fresh basil
6 tbsp	(90 ml) vegetable oil
1 tbsp	(15 ml) lemon juice

In a pot of boiling salted water, blanch the broccoli for 2 minutes. Drain. Plunge into ice water for 2 minutes. Drain.

In a food processor, finely chop the broccoli, Parmesan, pumpkin seeds, and basil. Add the oil in a steady stream and mix well. Using a spatula, scrape down the sides of the processor bowl a few times. Add the lemon juice. Season with salt and pepper.

Serve cold as a dip or hot with pasta. The pesto will keep for 1 week in an airtight container in the refrigerator or 6 months in the freezer. Top with a layer of olive oil to prevent the pesto from oxidizing.

NOTE *To serve with pasta, reserve 1/2 cup (125 ml) of the pasta cooking water to add to the pesto and toss to coat. Garnish with extra pumpkin seeds and basil leaves, if desired.*

PREPARATION	COOKING	MAKES	FREEZES
15 MIN	2 MIN	2 1/4 CUPS (560 ML)	YES

Broccoli Pesto

ARTICHOKE PESTO

1	jar (6 oz/170 ml) oil-packed artichokes, drained
1	garlic clove, sliced
1/2 cup	(35 g) freshly grated Parmesan cheese
1/2 cup	(15 g) flat-leaf parsley
1/4 cup	(35 g) toasted pine nuts
1/4 cup	(60 ml) vegetable oil

In a food processor, finely chop the artichokes, garlic, Parmesan, parsley, and pine nuts. Add the oil in a steady stream and mix well. Using a spatula, scrape down the sides of the processor bowl a few times. Season with salt and pepper.

Serve hot with pasta. The pesto will keep for 2 weeks in an airtight container in the refrigerator or 6 months in the freezer. Top with a layer of olive oil to prevent the pesto from oxidizing.

NOTE *To serve with pasta, reserve 1/2 cup (125 ml) of the pasta cooking water, add to the pesto, and toss to coat.*

PREPARATION	COOKING	MAKES	FREEZES
15 MIN	–	1 CUP (250 ML)	YES

TUSCAN KALE PESTO

2 cups	(80 g) Tuscan kale leaves (see note)
1	small garlic clove, sliced
1/2 cup	(35 g) freshly grated Parmesan cheese
1/4 cup	(35 g) unsalted shelled toasted pistachios
1/2 cup	(125 ml) olive oil
2 tsp	(10 ml) lemon juice

In a pot of boiling salted water, blanch the kale for 1 minute. Drain. Plunge into ice water for 2 minutes. Drain and then squeeze dry with a clean tea towel.

In a food processor, finely chop the kale, garlic, Parmesan, and pistachios. Add the oil in a steady stream and mix well. Using a spatula, scrape down the sides of the processor bowl a few times. Add the lemon juice. Season with salt and pepper.

Serve hot with pasta. The kale pesto will keep for 2 weeks in an airtight container in the refrigerator or 6 months in the freezer. Top with a layer of olive oil to prevent the pesto from oxidizing.

NOTE *You can replace the Tuscan kale with 2 cups (100 g) of curly kale. To serve with pasta, reserve 1/2 cup (125 ml) of the pasta cooking water, add to the pesto, and toss to coat.*

PREPARATION	COOKING	MAKES	FREEZES
15 MIN	1 MIN	1 CUP (250 ML)	YES

CAULIFLOWER COUSCOUS

1	cauliflower, cut into florets
1	onion, finely chopped
2	garlic cloves, finely chopped
2 tbsp	(30 ml) butter
1/2 tsp	ground coriander
1/2 tsp	ground cumin
1/4 tsp	ground turmeric
1/4 tsp	ground ginger
1/4 tsp	crushed red pepper flakes
1 cup	(250 ml) chicken broth
1/2 cup	(55 g) sliced almonds, toasted
1/4 cup	(30 g) currants
1	can (19 oz/540 ml) chickpeas, drained and rinsed
2 tbsp	(30 ml) lemon juice

In a food processor, chop the cauliflower, one-third at a time, until it is the size of large couscous. You'll have about 6 cups/1.5 L.

In a large non-stick skillet over medium heat, soften the onion and garlic in the butter. Add the spices and cook for 1 minute, stirring. Season with salt and pepper. Add the broth, almonds, and currants. Bring to a boil. Add the cauliflower and chickpeas. Cover and let simmer for 4 to 5 minutes or until the cauliflower is al dente. Add the lemon juice. Adjust the seasoning, if needed.

Delicious with grilled merguez sausage, chicken, or white fish.

PREPARATION	COOKING	SERVINGS	FREEZES
25 MIN	25 MIN	4 TO 6	–

CORN WITH COCONUT CURRY SAUCE

SAUCE

1	shallot, chopped
1 tbsp	(15 ml) vegetable oil
1	can (14 oz/398 ml) coconut milk
2 tbsp	(30 ml) peanut butter
1 tbsp	curry powder
1 tbsp	(15 ml) lime juice

CORN

8	ears corn
1/4 cup	(40 g) finely chopped peanuts
1/4 cup	(10 g) finely chopped cilantro
1	cherry pepper, deseeded and chopped
	Lime wedges, for serving

SAUCE

In a small pot over medium-high heat, soften the shallot in the oil. Whisk in the remaining ingredients. Bring to a boil. Let simmer for 5 minutes or until the sauce has thickened slightly. Season with salt and pepper. Keep warm.

CORN

Meanwhile, in a pot of boiling salted water, cook the corn for 5 minutes. Drain.

Place the corn on a serving platter and coat with the sauce. Garnish with the peanuts, cilantro, and cherry pepper. Serve with the lime wedges.

PREPARATION	COOKING	MAKES	FREEZES
15 MIN	15 MIN	8	–

Roasted Cauliflower
with Béchamel Sauce

Hasselback Squash

Grilled Broccoli
and Béarnaise Sauce

THINKING BIG
A WHOLE VEGETABLE AS A CENTREPIECE

BACK IN THE DAY, A WHOLE ROAST BEEF IN THE MIDDLE OF THE TABLE HAD
SERIOUS WOW FACTOR. NOW VEGETABLES CAN HEADLINE A MEAL AND
HAVE JUST AS MUCH IMPACT. IMAGINE A WHOLE GRILLED CAULIFLOWER
OR BROCCOLI SERVED ON A PLATTER, OR BUTTERNUT SQUASH PRESENTED
HASSELBACK-STYLE (FINELY SLICED WITHOUT CUTTING ALL THE WAY
THROUGH). TOPPED OFF WITH ONE OF THE FOUR SAUCES ON PAGES 86–87,
IT'S GUARANTEED TO STEAL THE SHOW.

ROASTED CAULIFLOWER

1	cauliflower, trimmed
2 tbsp	(30 ml) butter, melted

With the rack in the middle position, preheat the oven to 425°F (220°C).

In a large pot of boiling salted water, cook the cauliflower, stem up, until it is al dente, about 7 minutes. Drain well and place in a baking dish, stem down. Brush the cauliflower with the melted butter. Season with salt and pepper.

Bake for 10 minutes. Finish it under the broiler for 3 to 5 minutes or until the cauliflower is golden brown.

PREPARATION 5 MIN	**SERVINGS** 4 TO 6
COOKING 20 MIN	**FREEZES** –

GRILLED BROCCOLI

1	broccoli, stem peeled
2 tbsp	(30 ml) butter, melted

With the rack in the middle position, preheat the oven to broil.

In a large pot of boiling salted water, cook the broccoli until it is al dente, about 5 minutes. Drain well and place on its side in a baking dish. Brush the broccoli with the melted butter. Season with salt and pepper.

Bake for 5 minutes or until the broccoli begins to brown.

PREPARATION 10 MIN	**SERVINGS** 4 TO 6
COOKING 10 MIN	**FREEZES** –

HASSELBACK SQUASH

| 1 | butternut squash (about 2 lb/900 g) |
| 2 tbsp | (30 ml) olive oil |

With the rack in the middle position, preheat the oven to 400°F (200°C).

On a work surface, peel the squash using a vegetable peeler. Cut the squash in half lengthwise. Using a spoon, scoop out the seeds.

Place the squash halves cut-side down and score them without cutting all the way through (see note). Place in a glass baking dish. Drizzle the oil over top and season with salt and pepper. Cover tightly with aluminum foil.

Bake for 45 minutes or until the squash is al dente. Remove the foil and broil for 3 to 5 minutes or until light golden.

NOTE *To keep from cutting all the way through the squash, place chopsticks on either side of the squash—they will prevent the knife from cutting all the way to the base.*

PREPARATION	SERVINGS
15 MIN	4 TO 6
COOKING	**FREEZES**
50 MIN	–

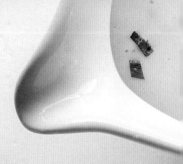

TRADITIONAL VINAIGRETTE

1/3 cup	(75 ml) vegetable oil
3 tbsp	(45 ml) apple cider vinegar
1 tsp	(5 ml) Dijon mustard
1 tsp	salt
1/4 tsp	(1 ml) honey
1/4 tsp	freshly ground pepper
1 small	garlic clove, finely chopped

In a bowl, whisk together all of the ingredients. Adjust the seasoning, if needed.

Delicious with a mix of lettuces, in coleslaw, or on hasselback squash (recipe p. 85).

NOTE *Add 3 tbsp (45 ml) of mayonnaise to this traditional vinaigrette for a creamy dressing.*

PREPARATION	MAKES
5 MIN	1/2 CUP (125 ML)
COOKING	FREEZES
–	–

Creamy Dressing

BÉARNAISE SAUCE

1/3 cup	(75 ml) white wine vinegar
2	sprigs fresh tarragon
1	shallot, chopped
1/2 tsp	crushed black peppercorns
3	egg yolks
3/4 cup	(170 g) butter, melted and cooled
1 tbsp	tarragon, finely chopped
1 tbsp	(15 ml) cold water

In a small pot, bring the vinegar, tarragon sprigs, shallot, and peppercorns to a boil. Let reduce by half. Pass through a fine sieve and discard any solids.

In the top of a double boiler, off the heat, whisk the vinegar reduction and egg yolks together. Place over simmering water and whisk until the mixture thickens and becomes frothy, about 4 to 5 minutes. Do not overcook the egg yolks.

Remove from the heat and whisk in the melted butter. Add the chopped tarragon and cold water. Season with salt and pepper.

Serve with grilled broccoli (recipe p. 84), or grilled salmon or beef.

PREPARATION	MAKES
15 MIN	1 1/4 CUPS (310 ML)
COOKING	FREEZES
8 MIN	–

Traditional Vinaigrette

Béarnaise Sauce

HOLLANDAISE SAUCE

3 tbsp	(45 ml) water
1 tbsp	(15 ml) white wine vinegar
3	egg yolks
3/4 cup	(170 g) butter, melted and cooled

In the top of a double boiler, off the heat, whisk together the water, vinegar, and egg yolks. Place over simmering water and whisk until the mixture thickens and becomes frothy, about 4 to 5 minutes. Do not overcook the egg yolks.

Remove from the heat and whisk in the melted butter. Season with salt and pepper.

Delicious with asparagus, steamed potatoes, or on eggs Benedict.

PREPARATION	MAKES
10 MIN	1 1/2 CUPS (375 ML)
COOKING	FREEZES
5 MIN	–

BÉCHAMEL SAUCE

1/4 cup	(55 g) butter
1/4 cup	(40 g) unbleached all-purpose flour
2 cups	(500 ml) milk
1	pinch ground nutmeg

In a pot over medium heat, melt the butter. Add the flour and cook for 1 minute, stirring. Add the milk and bring to a boil, whisking constantly. Let simmer for 5 minutes.

Remove from the heat and add the nutmeg. Season with salt and pepper.

Serve with roasted cauliflower (recipe p. 84), on pasta, or in a croque monsieur.

NOTE *For a Mornay sauce, add 1 1/2 cups (150 g) grated Gruyère cheese to the béchamel.*

PREPARATION	MAKES
5 MIN	2 CUPS (500 ML)
COOKING	FREEZES
10 MIN	–

Hollandaise Sauce

Béchamel Sauce

RÖSTI-STYLE POTATO WAFFLES

WAFFLES

3 lb	(1.4 kg) Russet potatoes, peeled (about 6 large potatoes)
1/4 cup	(55 g) salted butter, melted
1/2 tsp	salt
	Vegetable oil, for cooking

CHIVE CREAM

1 cup	(250 ml) sour cream
1/4 cup	(13 g) finely chopped chives
4 oz	(115 g) smoked salmon or gravlax

WAFFLES

Grate the potatoes. Place half of the grated potato at a time on a tea towel and wring out the excess liquid. You should have about 6 cups (1.5 L) of grated potato.

In a bowl, combine the potato, butter, and salt. Season to taste with pepper.

Preheat a Belgian-style waffle iron. Lightly oil it. Spread a quarter of the potato mixture at a time on the waffle iron. Close. Cook for 15 minutes or until the waffle is golden. Keep warm in an oven set at 200°F (95°C). Repeat with the remaining potato mixture.

CHIVE CREAM

Meanwhile, mix the sour cream and chives together in a bowl. Season to taste with salt and pepper.

Serve the hot waffles with the chive cream. Garnish with smoked salmon or gravlax. You can also serve them with poached eggs. For even more vegetables, add a few asparagus spears or fiddleheads, if they're in season.

PREPARATION	COOKING	SERVINGS	FREEZES
30 MIN	1 H	4	–

WEDGE SALAD

SALAD

8	slices bacon
3	eggs
4 cups	(200 g) stale bread cubes
3 tbsp	(40 g) butter
1	head iceberg lettuce, cut into quarters
2	tomatoes, cut into wedges
1/2 cup	(60 g) shaved Parmesan

VINAIGRETTE

1/2 cup	(35 g) freshly grated Parmesan cheese
1	egg yolk
1	small garlic clove, finely chopped
1 tbsp	(15 ml) Dijon mustard
1 tbsp	(15 ml) anchovy paste
2 tbsp	(30 ml) lemon juice
1 cup	(250 ml) canola oil

SALAD

With the rack in the middle position, preheat the oven to 400°F (200°C). Line a baking sheet with parchment paper.

Place the bacon on the baking sheet. Bake for 15 to 20 minutes or until the bacon is fully cooked and crispy. Drain on paper towel. Let cool and then cut into pieces.

Meanwhile, place the eggs in a small pot and cover with cold water. Bring to a boil. Once the water begins to boil, cover and remove from the heat. Let sit 10 minutes. Remove the eggs from the pot and plunge into ice water to stop the cooking process. Peel the eggs. Set aside in a bowl of cold water. Just before serving, dry the eggs and cut them into wedges.

In a non-stick skillet over medium heat, brown the bread cubes in the butter. Season with salt and pepper. Let cool.

VINAIGRETTE

In a bowl, whisk together the Parmesan, egg yolk, garlic, mustard, anchovy paste, and lemon juice. Add the oil in a steady stream, whisking all the while.

TO SERVE

Place the lettuce on plates. Add the tomatoes, bacon, eggs, and croutons. Drizzle with the vinaigrette. Sprinkle with the shaved Parmesan. Season with pepper.

PREPARATION	COOKING	SERVINGS	FREEZES
25 MIN	25 MIN	4	–

KANI SALAD

LEMON MAYONNAISE
1/2 cup	(125 ml) mayonnaise
1 tbsp	(15 ml) lemon juice
1 tsp	chopped pickled ginger
1/4 tsp	Espelette pepper
1/4 tsp	finely grated orange zest

SALAD
3 oz	(85 g) rice vermicelli
3	carrots, julienned
2	Lebanese cucumbers, julienned
1/2	iceberg lettuce, sliced
1/2 lb	(225 g) crab meat, imitation crab, or lobster meat, shredded
1/4	sheet nori, sliced (optional)

LEMON MAYONNAISE

In a bowl, whisk together all of the ingredients. Season with salt and pepper. Refrigerate until ready to serve.

SALAD

Place the rice noodles in a pot of boiling water. Remove from the heat and let sit for 3 minutes to soften the noodles. Drain and rinse under cold running water. Drain well. Cut the noodles to shorten them.

Add the vegetables, crab, and lemon mayonnaise. Adjust the seasoning.

Transfer the salad to plates and garnish with the nori, if desired. Serve immediately.

PREPARATION	COOKING	SERVINGS	FREEZES
35 MIN	3 MIN	4	–

ENDIVE SALAD
WITH BLOOD ORANGES

DRESSING

1/4 cup	(60 ml) mayonnaise
2 tbsp	(30 ml) white wine vinegar
1 tbsp	(15 ml) whole-grain mustard
1 tbsp	(15 ml) honey
1	small garlic clove, finely chopped

SALAD

4 cups	(100 g) torn Boston lettuce leaves
2	white endives, leaves separated and cut in half diagonally
2	red endives, leaves separated and cut in half diagonally, or a small radicchio
2	blood oranges, supremed (see note)
1/2 cup	(50 g) toasted walnuts, chopped

DRESSING

In a bowl, whisk together all of the ingredients. Season with salt and pepper.

SALAD

Place the Boston lettuce on plates with the endives. Add the oranges and walnuts.

Just before serving, drizzle the salad with the dressing and toss to combine.

Can be served as an appetizer or as a side for pasta with Bolognese sauce, meat, or poultry.

NOTE *To supreme the oranges, trim the two ends of each orange and place cut-side down on a work surface. Using a knife, and getting as close as possible to the orange flesh, remove all the pith and skin of the oranges. Slide the blade of the knife between each segment and remove them from the membrane.*

PREPARATION	COOKING	SERVINGS	FREEZES
20 MIN	–	4 TO 6	–

FAMILY MATTERS

I taught my three daughters how to taste. They had the right not to like something, but they had to give it a chance first. Given that it can take as many as ten tries before we learn to like a new food, cooking it differently the second time around can increase the chances of success. I also showed them how to eat at the table with family and friends, how to take their time, and how to give others time to enjoy a meal. Ultimately, that's my recipe for fighting the rise of individualism and the fast pace of life. We know that vegetables can work miracles for us, but finding varied ways to eat them each day can be challenging. Sitting down for a family meal should be all about creating a shared moment together, and that means recipes that win over the whole table.

VEGETABLE BOLOGNESE

2	carrots
2	celery stalks
1	onion
1	medium eggplant
6 oz	(170 g) portobello mushrooms
1/4 cup	(55 g) unsalted butter
2	anchovy fillets, chopped
1/3 cup	(75 ml) red wine
1/4 cup	(60 ml) tomato paste
2 cups	(500 ml) vegetable or chicken broth
1 cup	(250 ml) tomato purée
2	bay leaves
1	pinch crushed red pepper flakes
1/2 cup	(125 ml) milk
1	garlic clove, chopped
1 tsp	finely chopped fresh rosemary
1 lb	(450 g) pappardelle noodles
	Freshly grated Parmesan cheese, for serving

On a work surface, roughly chop all of the vegetables.

In a food processor, finely chop the carrots, celery, and onion together. Set aside in a bowl. Next, finely chop the eggplant, then the mushrooms.

In a large pot over high heat, cook all of the vegetables together in the butter until they begin to colour and the liquid has evaporated. Season with salt and pepper. Add the anchovies and cook for 1 minute, stirring.

Deglaze with the wine and let reduce to almost dry. Add the tomato paste and cook for 1 minute, stirring. Add the broth, tomato purée, bay leaves, and red pepper flakes. Bring to a boil. Cover, turn down the heat, and let simmer for 1 hour, stirring occasionally.

Remove the lid and add the milk. Simmer for another 30 minutes, stirring occasionally. Add the garlic and rosemary. Adjust the seasoning.

Meanwhile, in a pot of boiling salted water, cook the pasta until it is al dente. Reserve 1 cup (250 ml) of the cooking water. Drain the pasta.

Add the pasta to the sauce. Warm through for 2 minutes, stirring to coat the pasta in sauce. Add the cooking water to thin out the sauce, as needed. Serve with Parmesan.

NOTE *Allow about 2.5 oz (75 g) of pasta and 1 cup (250 ml) of sauce per person. This recipe makes 6 cups (1.5 L) of sauce.*

PREPARATION	COOKING	SERVINGS	FREEZES
20 MIN	2 H	6	SAUCE ONLY

PORTOBELLO MUSHROOM AND JERK CHICKEN

4	green onions, roughly chopped
2	bird's eye chilies
1	garlic clove, chopped
1/4 cup	(60 ml) apple cider vinegar
1/4 cup	(60 ml) maple syrup
2 tbsp	(30 ml) dark rum
2 tbsp	(30 ml) soy sauce
1/2 tsp	dried oregano
1/2 tsp	ground allspice
1/2 tsp	ground cumin
1/4 tsp	ground cinnamon
8	chicken thighs, boneless and skinless
4	portobello mushrooms, peeled

In a blender, purée the green onions, chilies, garlic, vinegar, maple syrup, rum, soy sauce, and spices.

Place the chicken and mushrooms in a glass baking dish or sealable bag. Add the marinade and toss to coat. Cover the dish or close the bag. Let marinate in the refrigerator for 8 hours or overnight.

Preheat the grill to high. Oil the grate.

Drain the chicken and mushrooms, reserving the marinade. Lightly salt the chicken and mushrooms.

Grill the chicken and mushrooms for 5 minutes. Brush lightly with the reserved marinade and discard any leftovers. Continue grilling for 5 more minutes or until the chicken is fully cooked.

Delicious with a green salad or in a sandwich.

PREPARATION	MARINATING	COOKING	SERVINGS	FREEZES
20 MIN	8 H	10 MIN	4	–

MINESTRONE

1	carrot, diced
1	celery stalk, diced
1	small onion, chopped
1	garlic clove, chopped
1/4 tsp	crushed red pepper flakes
2 tbsp	(30 ml) olive oil, plus more for serving
4 cups	(1 L) chicken broth
1 cup	(250 ml) tomato purée
2 cups	(170 g) Savoy cabbage, roughly chopped
1	large potato, peeled and diced
1	can (19 oz/540 ml) white beans, drained and rinsed
	Celery leaves, for serving

In a large pot over medium-high heat, soften the carrot, celery, onion, garlic, and red pepper flakes in the oil for 5 minutes. Add the broth, tomato purée, cabbage, potato, and beans. Season with salt and pepper. Bring to a boil. Cover, turn down the heat, and let simmer for 20 minutes or until the soup thickens and the vegetables are tender. Adjust the seasoning.

Just before serving, drizzle with olive oil. Garnish with celery leaves and freshly ground pepper.

PREPARATION	COOKING	SERVINGS	FREEZES
25 MIN	30 MIN	4 TO 6	YES

CHICKEN-FREE POT PIE

FILLING

1 tbsp	unbleached all-purpose flour
3 tbsp	(40 g) butter, softened
1	onion, finely chopped
1	garlic clove, finely chopped
2 1/2 cups	(625 ml) chicken broth
2 cups	(325 g) mix of 1/4-inch (5 mm) rounds of carrot and parsnip
2 cups	(300 g) peeled and diced sweet potato (about 1 medium sweet potato)
1 cup	(160 g) peeled and diced potato (about 1 potato)
1 cup	(150 g) frozen peas

DOUGH

1 1/4 cups	(190 g) unbleached all-purpose flour
2 tsp	baking powder
1/2 tsp	salt
1/2 cup	(115 g) unsalted butter, cold and cubed
3/4 cup	(180 ml) buttermilk, cold

FILLING

In a bowl, mix the flour with 2 tbsp (30 ml) of the butter. Set aside.

In a pot over medium heat, brown the onion and garlic in the remaining butter. Add the broth, carrot and parsnip mix, sweet potato, and potato. Bring to a boil. Cover and let simmer for 5 minutes. Whisk in the butter-flour mixture and whisk to combine. Bring to a boil. Add the peas. Season with salt and pepper. Transfer the mixture to an 11- x 8-inch (28 x 20 cm) baking dish. Set aside.

With the rack in the middle position, preheat the oven to 400°F (200°C).

DOUGH

In a food processor, mix the flour, baking powder, and salt. Add the butter and pulse until the butter is in pea-sized pieces. Add the buttermilk and pulse until the dough just comes together. The dough will be quite soft. Using a 2 tbsp (30 ml) ice cream scoop, place balls of the dough on top of the vegetable mixture.

Bake for 30 minutes or until the dough is golden and a toothpick inserted into the centre of a piece of dough comes out clean.

PREPARATION	COOKING	SERVINGS	FREEZES
30 MIN	50 MIN	6	YES

Grilled Vegetable
and Salmon Salad

GRILLED VEGETABLE AND SALMON SALAD

SALMON

3 tbsp	(45 ml) whisky or bourbon
1 tbsp	brown sugar
1 tbsp	(15 ml) molasses
1 tbsp	(15 ml) whole-grain mustard
1 tbsp	(15 ml) vegetable oil
1 lb	(450 g) fillet of salmon, skin-on, cut into 4 pieces

MUSTARD MAYONNAISE

1/4 cup	(60 ml) mayonnaise
1 tbsp	(15 ml) whole-grain mustard
1 tbsp	(15 ml) water

GRILLED VEGETABLES

3/4 lb	(340 g) baby potatoes, cut in half
3/4 lb	(340 g) asparagus, trimmed
6	green onions, cut in half lengthwise
2 tbsp	(30 ml) vegetable oil
3	radishes, sliced
1 cup	(30 g) watercress

SALMON

In a glass baking dish, whisk together all of the ingredients except the salmon. Season with salt and pepper.

Place the salmon in the marinade and toss to coat. Cover and refrigerate for 4 to 8 hours. Drain and dry the fillets. Set aside on a plate.

MUSTARD MAYONNAISE

In a bowl, whisk together all of the ingredients. Season with salt and pepper. Cover and refrigerate until ready to serve.

GRILLED VEGETABLES

Place a grill wok on the barbeque. Preheat the grill to medium-high. Oil the grate beside the grill wok for the salmon.

Coat the vegetables with oil. Season with salt and pepper. Grill the potatoes in the wok for 10 minutes. Add the asparagus and green onions, and continue cooking for 5 to 8 minutes or until the vegetables are tender, stirring occasionally.

Meanwhile, grill the salmon skin-side down for 6 minutes, flipping halfway through the cooking time. It will be medium-rare.

Transfer the vegetables to plates, and top with the salmon, radishes, and watercress. Drizzle with the mustard mayonnaise.

PREPARATION	MARINATING	COOKING	SERVINGS	FREEZES
30 MIN	4 H	15 MIN	4	–

ROOT VEGETABLE GRATIN

2 cups	(450 g) peeled and grated Russet potatoes
3 cups	(450 g) mix of peeled and grated root vegetables (carrots, parsnip, kohlrabi, celeriac)
6	green onions, finely chopped
1 cup	(250 ml) crème fraîche
2 1/2 cups	(250 g) grated Edam or mozzarella cheese

With the rack in the middle position, preheat the oven to 400°F (200°C). Butter an 11- x 8-inch (28 x 20 cm) baking dish with an 8-cup (2 L) capacity.

In a bowl, combine the vegetables with the crème fraîche and 2 cups (200 g) of the cheese. Transfer to the baking dish and press down on the mixture slightly. Sprinkle with the remaining cheese.

Bake for 45 minutes or until the vegetables are tender and golden brown. Let rest for 10 minutes before serving.

Delicious with roast beef or a leg of lamb.

PREPARATION	COOKING	SERVINGS	FREEZES
35 MIN	45 MIN	8	–

Eggplant Parmesan

EGGPLANT PARMESAN

EGGPLANT

2	large eggplants
1/4 cup	(60 ml) olive oil

PARMESAN BREADCRUMBS

1/4 cup	(30 g) breadcrumbs
2 tbsp	(30 ml) butter
1/4 cup	(20 g) freshly grated Parmesan cheese

TOPPING

1 1/2 cups	(375 ml) tomato sauce, hot (recipe p. 239)
1 cup	(100 g) grated mozzarella cheese
1/4 cup	(20 g) freshly grated Parmesan cheese
2 tbsp	(30 ml) torn basil leaves

EGGPLANT

With the rack in the middle position, preheat the oven to 375°F (190°C). Line a baking sheet with a silicone mat or parchment paper.

On a work surface, cut the eggplants in half lengthwise. Using a paring knife, score the flesh of the eggplants without piercing through the skin. Season with salt and pepper.

In a large non-stick skillet over medium-high heat, brown the eggplants in the oil, cut-side down only. Transfer to the baking sheet, cut-side up. Bake for 40 minutes or until the flesh of the eggplants is tender. Set aside.

PARMESAN BREADCRUMBS

Meanwhile, in a small non-stick skillet over medium heat, toast the breadcrumbs in the butter. Remove from the heat and add the Parmesan. Mix to combine and let cool.

TOPPING

Spread the tomato sauce on top of the eggplants. Top with the mozzarella and Parmesan. Bake for 10 minutes or until the cheese is melted. Let cool for 10 minutes. Sprinkle the breadcrumbs and basil over top.

Delicious as a main dish. You can also serve alongside grilled meat cutlets.

PREPARATION	COOKING	SERVINGS	FREEZES
30 MIN	1 H	4	–

Red Soup

Green Soup

White Soup

RED SOUP
beets and red kidney beans

4	beets, peeled and diced
2	carrots, grated
1	onion, chopped
2	garlic cloves, chopped
2 tbsp	(30 ml) olive oil, plus more for serving
5 cups	(1.25 L) beef broth
1/4 cup	(60 ml) dill pickle juice
1	can (19 oz/540 ml) red kidney beans, drained and rinsed

In a large pot over medium heat, cook the vegetables in the oil for 10 minutes. Add the broth, pickle juice, and beans. Season with salt and pepper. Bring to a boil, turn down the heat, and let simmer for 30 minutes or until the vegetables are tender. Adjust the seasoning.

Just before serving, drizzle with olive oil and season with pepper.

PREPARATION	COOKING	SERVINGS	FREEZES
25 MIN	35 MIN	6	YES

GREEN SOUP

cabbage, avocado, cilantro, chicken

4	green onions, chopped (green and white parts separated)
2	garlic cloves, chopped
2 tbsp	(30 ml) olive oil
4 cups	(340 g) sliced green cabbage
4	thin slices fresh ginger
1	lemongrass stalk, crushed
1	small jalapeño pepper, deseeded and finely sliced
4 cups	(1 L) chicken broth
2 tbsp	(30 ml) soy sauce
2 cups	(340 g) shredded cooked chicken
1 cup	(50 g) finely chopped cilantro
1	avocado, diced and sprinkled with lime juice
	Lime wedges, for serving

In a large pot over medium-high heat, soften the white parts of the green onion with the garlic in the oil for 2 minutes. Add the cabbage, ginger, lemongrass, jalapeño, broth, and soy sauce. Season lightly with salt and pepper. Bring to a boil, cover, turn down the heat, and let simmer for 10 minutes or until the vegetables are tender. Remove the ginger and lemongrass. The soup can be frozen at this point.

Just before serving, add the green parts of the green onion, the chicken, and the cilantro. Season with salt and pepper. Garnish with the avocado and lime wedges.

NOTE *If you like spicy soups, slice the jalapeño without deseeding it.*

PREPARATION	COOKING	SERVINGS	FREEZES
30 MIN	25 MIN	6	YES

WHITE SOUP

leek, potato, clams

2	leeks, whites only, sliced
2	garlic cloves, chopped
2	slices bacon, chopped
1/4 cup	(55 g) butter
2 tbsp	(30 ml) unbleached all-purpose flour
4 cups	(1 L) chicken broth
1	can (142 g) small clams, liquid and clams separated
4	potatoes, peeled and diced
1/2 cup	(125 ml) 35% cream

In a large pot over medium heat, soften the leek, garlic, and bacon in the butter for 10 minutes. Add the flour and cook for 1 minute, stirring. Add the broth, clam water, and potatoes. Season with salt and pepper. Bring to a boil, turn down the heat, and let simmer for 20 minutes or until the vegetables are tender. Add the cream and the clams. Adjust the seasoning.

Just before serving, drizzle with olive oil and sprinkle with freshly ground pepper.

PREPARATION	COOKING	SERVINGS	FREEZES
20 MIN	30 MIN	6	YES

PEA RISOTTO

6 cups	(1.5 L) chicken broth
1	onion, chopped
2	garlic cloves, chopped
3 tbsp	(40 g) butter
1 1/2 cups	(315 g) arborio or carnaroli rice
1 cup	(250 ml) white wine
4 cups	(600 g) frozen peas, thawed
1 cup	(70 g) freshly grated Parmesan cheese
	Parmesan shavings, for serving

In a pot, bring the broth to a boil. Keep warm.

In a large pot over medium-high heat, soften the onion and garlic in half of the butter. Add the rice and cook for 1 minute, stirring constantly to coat the rice. Add the white wine and reduce almost to dry.

Over medium heat, add the broth, about 1 cup (250 ml) at a time, stirring frequently, until the liquid has almost entirely evaporated between each addition. Cook for 18 to 22 minutes or until the rice is al dente. Season with salt and pepper. Add more broth as needed.

Remove from the heat and add the peas, grated Parmesan, and the remaining butter. Mix well until the texture is creamy and the peas are hot. Adjust the seasoning, if needed.

Garnish with Parmesan shavings. Serve as an appetizer or main dish.

PREPARATION	COOKING	SERVINGS	FREEZES
40 MIN	30 MIN	4 TO 6	–

MUSHROOM STEW WITH PORK CUTLETS

MUSHROOM STEW

2	slices bacon, diced
1 lb	(450 g) white button mushrooms, cut in half
1/2 lb	(225 g) mixed mushrooms (shiitakes, creminis, portobellos), chopped
1	onion, chopped
2	garlic cloves, chopped
2 tbsp	(30 ml) tomato paste
1/2 cup	(125 ml) red wine
2 cups	(500 ml) beef broth
1 tsp	(5 ml) cornstarch
2 tbsp	(30 ml) water
1/4 cup	(13 g) finely chopped chives

PORK

1 lb	(450 g) small pork loin cutlets
1/4 cup	(40 g) unbleached all-purpose flour
1/4 cup	(55 g) butter

MUSHROOM STEW

In a pot over medium-high heat, brown the bacon. Add the mushrooms, onion, and garlic. Season with salt and pepper. Cook until the liquid has evaporated. Add the tomato paste and cook for 2 minutes, stirring. Deglaze with the wine and let reduce by half. Add the broth and let simmer for 10 minutes.

In a small bowl, dissolve the cornstarch in the water. Add it to the stew in a steady stream, stirring all the while. Cook for 5 minutes. Keep warm.

PORK

Meanwhile, on a work surface, place the cutlets between two pieces of plastic wrap and flatten them out using a mallet or rolling pin. Season with salt and pepper.

Place the flour on a large plate. Toss the cutlets in the flour and shake to remove any excess.

In a large skillet over high heat, brown two or three cutlets at a time in the butter. Season with salt and pepper. Add butter as needed.

Serve the cutlets with the mushroom stew. Sprinkle with chives. Delicious with corn polenta (recipe p. 127).

PREPARATION	COOKING	SERVINGS	FREEZES
35 MIN	40 MIN	4	–

CORN POLENTA

2	ears corn
3 1/2 cups	(825 ml) chicken broth
3/4 cup	(135 g) instant polenta
3/4 cup	(55 g) freshly grated Parmesan cheese

In a pot of boiling salted water, cook the ears of corn for 5 minutes. Drain. Rinse under cold running water. Using a knife, remove the kernels from the cob.

In another pot, bring the broth to a boil. Add the polenta in a steady stream, whisking constantly. Let simmer over low heat for 2 to 3 minutes, stirring frequently with a wooden spoon. Remove from the heat and add the Parmesan and corn kernels. Season with salt and pepper.

Serve as a side dish with cutlets, lamb, or sausages.

NOTE *If you cannot find ears of corn, substitute 2 cups (300 g) frozen corn kernels, thawed.*

PREPARATION	COOKING	SERVINGS	FREEZES
15 MIN	10 MIN	4	–

Vegetable Pizzas with Parmesan

VEGETABLE PIZZAS WITH PARMESAN

PARMESAN AND LEMON CREAM

3/4 cup	(180 ml) 35% cream
1/2 cup	(35 g) freshly grated Parmesan cheese
1 tbsp	(15 ml) lemon juice
1/4 tsp	crushed red pepper flakes
1	small garlic clove, finely chopped

PIZZAS

1	zucchini
1	red onion, cut into 1/4-inch (5 mm) slices
1	bell pepper, any colour, deseeded and cut into 1/4-inch (5 mm) slices
3 oz	(85 g) oyster mushrooms, torn into pieces
2 tbsp	(30 ml) olive oil
1	recipe pizza dough (recipe at right)
1	large beefsteak tomato, cut into 1/4-inch (5 mm) slices
2 tbsp	pitted black olives, cut lengthwise into quarters
1/2 cup	(35 g) freshly grated Parmesan cheese

PARMESAN AND LEMON CREAM

In a bowl, whisk together all of the ingredients. Set aside.

PIZZAS

Place a baking stone on a rack in the bottom position in the oven. You can also use an upside-down baking sheet. Preheat the oven to 450°F (230°C).

On a work surface, cut the zucchini in two lengthwise. Using a mandoline or vegetable peeler, cut the zucchini into long ribbons.

In a bowl, combine the zucchini, onion, bell pepper, and mushrooms with the oil. Season with salt and pepper.

Divide the pizza dough into four. On a lightly floured work surface, roll out one piece of dough at a time to an 8-inch (20 cm) disc. Place on a piece of parchment paper. Repeat with the remaining dough.

Spread the Parmesan and lemon cream on the dough. Cover with the tomato slices, the mixed vegetables, olives, and Parmesan. Bake one pizza at a time directly on the baking stove for 12 to 15 minutes or until the dough is cooked and golden brown.

PREPARATION	COOKING	SERVINGS	FREEZES
35 MIN	50 MIN	4	–

PIZZA DOUGH

2 1/4 cups	(340 g) unbleached all-purpose flour
1 tbsp	sugar
1 tsp	instant yeast
1/2 tsp	salt
1 cup	(250 ml) warm water

In a large bowl, using a wooden spoon, or in the bowl of a stand mixer fitted with the dough hook, mix the flour, sugar, yeast, and salt together. Add the water and mix until the dough comes together. Knead the dough for 5 minutes on a floured work surface, or continue mixing with the dough hook, until the dough is smooth.

Shape into a ball and place in a lightly oiled bowl, turning the dough over to coat with the oil. Cover with a damp cloth and let rise in a warm, humid place for 2 hours or until the dough doubles in volume.

PREPARATION	RISING	MAKES	FREEZES
15 MIN	2 H	4 PIZZAS	YES

SWISS CHARD WITH VEAL MEATBALLS

1 lb	(450 g) lean ground veal
1/4 cup	(30 g) breadcrumbs
1	egg
2 tbsp	(30 ml) sun-dried tomato pesto
1/4 tsp	salt
2	bunches Swiss chard (about 14 oz/400 g)
2 tbsp	(30 ml) olive oil
6	garlic cloves, chopped
1/4 cup	(30 g) pine nuts

In a bowl, combine the veal, breadcrumbs, egg, pesto, and salt. Season with pepper. With lightly oiled hands, shape the mixture into 1 tbsp (15 ml) balls. Set aside on a plate.

Separate the leaves and stems of the Swiss chard. Slice the stems and place in a bowl. Roughly chop the leaves and place in another bowl.

In a large non-stick skillet over high heat, brown the meatballs in the oil. Add the garlic and pine nuts. Continue cooking for 2 minutes or until the pine nuts are golden. Add the Swiss chard stems and continue cooking for 3 minutes until the stems are al dente. Add the leaves, cover the pan, and cook for 3 minutes or until the leaves are wilted. Season with salt and pepper.

Serve on a platter with couscous or mashed potatoes.

PREPARATION	COOKING	SERVINGS	FREEZES
40 MIN	15 MIN	6	–

SPANISH OMELETTE

OMELETTE

4	medium yellow-fleshed potatoes, peeled
6 tbsp	(90 ml) canola oil
2 oz	(55 g) chorizo, diced
1	onion, chopped
1	garlic clove, chopped
8	eggs

SALAD

2 cups	(50 g) arugula
1 tbsp	(15 ml) olive oil
1 tsp	(5 ml) sherry vinegar

OMELETTE

Using a spiralizer, cut the potatoes into large spirals (or cut into thin slices with a knife). Dry with paper towel.

With the rack in the middle position, preheat the oven to 350°F (180°C).

In a large ovenproof non-stick skillet over medium-high heat, cook the potatoes in the oil with the chorizo, onion, and garlic until tender, about 10 minutes. Season with salt and pepper. Drain the potato-onion mixture in a sieve set over a bowl. Reserve 3 tbsp (45 ml) of the oil.

Meanwhile, whisk the eggs in a bowl. Season with salt and pepper.

In the same skillet over medium heat, warm the reserved oil. Transfer the potato-onion mixture to the skillet. Add the eggs and gently stir to combine. Cook for 2 minutes. Remove from the heat and place in the oven for 15 minutes or until the omelette is cooked. Slide the omelette onto a large plate.

SALAD

In a bowl, combine all of the ingredients. Season with salt and pepper. Garnish with the salad.

Serve warm or cold, for brunch or lunch.

PREPARATION	COOKING	SERVINGS	FREEZES
10 MIN	30 MIN	4 TO 6	OMELETTE ONLY

FISH WITH CORN BEURRE BLANC

1 1/2 cups	(225 g) frozen corn kernels, thawed or 2 ears corn, cooked and kernels cut off the cob
1/2 cup	(115 g) butter, softened
1/4 cup	(60 ml) white wine
1/4 cup	(60 ml) white wine vinegar
1	shallot, finely chopped
1/4 cup	(60 ml) 35% cream
1 1/2 lb	(675 g) cod fillet, cut into 4 pieces
3 tbsp	(45 ml) vegetable oil
1 tbsp	(15 ml) finely chopped chives
3/4 lb	(340 g) flat or regular green beans, trimmed and blanched for 2 minutes

In a food processor, chop 1 cup (150 g) of the corn kernels. Add the butter and process until smooth. Set aside.

In a small pot, bring the wine, vinegar, and shallots to a boil. Let reduce to 2 tbsp (30 ml). Add the cream and cook for 2 minutes over medium heat.

Remove from the heat and add the corn-butter mixture, whisking all the while. Pass through a sieve, pressing on the solids with the back of a ladle to extract all the liquid. Return the liquid to the pot and heat for 2 minutes, stirring. Cover and keep warm.

Meanwhile, in a large non-stick skillet over medium-high heat, cook the fish in 2 tbsp (30 ml) of the oil for 3 to 5 minutes per side, depending on the thickness of the fillets. Season with salt and pepper. Keep warm. Wipe out the skillet.

In the same skillet, heat the remaining corn in the remaining oil for 2 minutes, stirring. Remove from the heat. Add the chives. Season with salt and pepper.

Drizzle the sauce over the fish. Top with the corn kernels. Serve with the green beans.

PREPARATION	COOKING	SERVINGS	FREEZES
20 MIN	25 MIN	4	–

RED COCONUT CURRY SOUP

4	green onions, sliced (white and green parts separated)
2	garlic cloves, chopped
1 tbsp	fresh ginger, finely chopped
1	bird's eye chili, whole
2 tbsp	(30 ml) vegetable oil
2 tbsp	(30 ml) red curry paste
4 cups	(1 L) chicken broth
1	can (14 oz/398 ml) coconut milk
1/2 lb	(225 g) bok choy (leaves and stems separated, stems sliced)
2	carrots, thinly sliced
1 tbsp	(15 ml) brown sugar
1 tbsp	(15 ml) fish sauce (nuoc mam)
1	red bell pepper, deseeded and thinly sliced
2 tbsp	(30 ml) lime juice
5 oz	(140 g) thick rice vermicelli (see note)
2 cups	(150 g) bean sprouts
1/4 cup	(10 g) Thai basil or cilantro
	Lime wedges, for serving

In a large pot, brown the white parts of the green onions, garlic, ginger, and chili in the oil. Season with salt and pepper. Add the curry paste and cook for 30 seconds, stirring. Add the broth, coconut milk, bok choy stems, carrots, brown sugar, and fish sauce. Bring to a boil and let simmer for 5 minutes or until the carrots are al dente. Add the bok choy leaves, bell pepper, and lime juice. Let simmer for 1 minute. Adjust the seasoning. Remove the chili, if desired.

Meanwhile, plunge the rice vermicelli into a pot of boiling water. Remove from the heat and let sit for 3 to 5 minutes or until the vermicelli is tender. Drain.

Transfer the vermicelli and bean sprouts to bowls. Cover with the soup. Top with the Thai basil and green parts of the green onions. Serve with lime wedges.

NOTE *For this soup, we used thicker rice noodles. For a main course soup, add 3/4 lb (340 g) soft tofu or 3/4 lb (340 g) medium shrimp, cooked and peeled, to the soup before serving.*

PREPARATION	COOKING	SERVINGS	FREEZES
20 MIN	15 MIN	4	–

Cauliflower Satay

CAULIFLOWER SATAY

SATAY SAUCE

3/4 cup	(180 ml) coconut milk
1/2 cup	(125 ml) peanut butter
1/4 cup	(60 ml) lime juice
2 tbsp	(30 ml) honey
1 tbsp	(15 ml) sambal oelek
1 tbsp	(15 ml) soy sauce

CAULIFLOWER

1/2 cup	(125 ml) plain Greek yogurt
2 tbsp	(30 ml) peanut butter
1 tbsp	(15 ml) honey
1 tsp	ground cumin
1 tsp	(5 ml) sambal oelek
2	garlic cloves, chopped
1	cauliflower, cut into florets

GARNISH

1	head Boston lettuce, leaves removed
1	English cucumber, julienned
1	carrot, julienned
2	green onions, sliced
1/4 cup	(40 g) chopped peanuts
1/4 cup	(10 g) cilantro leaves

SATAY SAUCE

In a small pot, bring all of the ingredients to a boil, whisking constantly. Let simmer for 2 minutes or until the sauce thickens. Transfer to a bowl. Cover and let cool. Stir before serving.

CAULIFLOWER

With the rack in the middle position, preheat the oven to 450°F (230°C).

In a bowl, whisk together the yogurt, peanut butter, honey, cumin, sambal oelek, and garlic. Add the cauliflower and toss to coat in the marinade. Transfer the cauliflower to a non-stick baking sheet or a sheet lined with aluminum foil.

Bake for 15 to 20 minutes or until the cauliflower is tender, turning the florets partway through cooking. Finish under the broiler for 3 minutes.

Transfer the cauliflower to a serving platter alongside the lettuce leaves, cucumber, carrot, green onion, peanuts, cilantro, and satay sauce. Everyone can garnish their own lettuce leaves.

PREPARATION	COOKING	SERVINGS	FREEZES
35 MIN	25 MIN	4	–

NAPA CABBAGE WITH SESAME

1 1/2 lb	(675 g) napa cabbage, sliced
1 tbsp	(15 ml) toasted sesame oil
1 tbsp	(15 ml) vegetable oil
2 tbsp	toasted white or black sesame seeds

In a large non-stick skillet over high heat, cook the cabbage in both oils for 5 minutes or until tender. Season with salt and pepper.

Transfer to a serving platter and sprinkle with the sesame seeds.

Serve with grilled fish, tofu, or pork.

PREPARATION	SERVINGS
5 MIN	4
COOKING	**FREEZES**
5 MIN	–

VEGETABLE TERIYAKI WITH GRILLED SHRIMP

SAUCE

1/4 cup	(60 ml) hoisin sauce
1/4 cup	(60 ml) vegetable broth (recipe p. 234)
2 tbsp	(30 ml) rice vinegar
2 tbsp	(30 ml) soy sauce
1 tbsp	brown sugar
2 tsp	cornstarch
1 tsp	(5 ml) sambal oelek

GRILLED SHRIMP

3/4 lb	(340 g) shrimp, peeled and deveined

SAUTÉ

1 tbsp	(15 ml) vegetable oil
1 tbsp	(15 ml) toasted sesame oil
1/2 lb	(225 g) snow peas, trimmed and cut in half lengthwise (or frozen shelled edamame, thawed)
6	green onions, sliced (white and green parts separated)
2	garlic cloves, chopped
1	carrot, julienned
1	red bell pepper, deseeded and cut into thin strips
1 tbsp	chopped fresh ginger
1/4 cup	(10 g) cilantro leaves

SAUCE

In a bowl, whisk together all of the ingredients.

GRILLED SHRIMP

Thread the shrimp onto small skewers. Brush with a bit of the sauce. Heat a cast iron grill pan on high heat until very hot. Oil the pan. Grill the skewers for 2 to 3 minutes per side or until the shrimp are cooked. Season with salt and pepper. Keep warm.

SAUTÉ

In a wok over high heat, heat both oils. Add the snow peas, the white parts of the green onion, garlic, carrot, bell pepper, and ginger and sauté for 4 minutes or until the vegetables begin to colour. Add the remaining sauce. Cook for 1 to 2 minutes or until the sauce is syrupy. Sprinkle with the green parts of the green onions and the cilantro.

Serve the vegetables and grilled shrimp skewers on a bed of rice or napa cabbage with sesame (recipe p. 145).

PREPARATION	COOKING	SERVINGS	FREEZES
25 MIN	20 MIN	4	–

LENTIL STEW
WITH CABBAGE STEAKS

LENTIL STEW

1	onion, chopped
2	garlic cloves, chopped
1	celery stalk, chopped
2 tbsp	(30 ml) vegetable oil
1 cup	(215 g) green lentils, drained and rinsed
2 cups	(500 ml) vegetable broth (recipe p. 234)
1	can (14 oz/398 ml) diced tomatoes
1 cup	(250 ml) tomato purée
1 tsp	dried oregano
1 tsp	dried mustard
1/2 tsp	celery salt
1/2 cup	(100 g) long-grain rice, drained and rinsed
1/4 cup	(10 g) finely chopped flat-leaf parsley

CABBAGE STEAKS

1/2	small green cabbage
2 tbsp	(30 ml) butter
1 cup	(250 ml) vegetable broth (recipe p. 234)

LENTIL STEW

In a large skillet over medium-high heat, brown the onion, garlic, and celery in the oil. Add the lentils, vegetable broth, canned tomatoes, tomato purée, oregano, mustard, and celery salt. Season with salt and pepper. Bring to a boil. Cover, turn down the heat, and let simmer for 10 minutes. Mix in the rice. Cover and let simmer for 20 minutes or until the rice is al dente. Let rest for 5 minutes, uncovered.

CABBAGE STEAKS

Meanwhile, on a work surface, cut the half cabbage into six wedges about 1 1/2 inches (4 cm) thick, leaving the core intact to hold the cabbage together while it cooks.

In another large non-stick skillet over medium-high heat, brown the cabbage wedges on one side in the butter. Season with salt and pepper. Turn the cabbage wedges over and add the broth. Bring to a boil. Cover and let simmer for 15 minutes. Uncover and continue cooking over high heat until the broth evaporates and the cabbage is al dente and golden brown, about 5 minutes.

Serve the lentil stew on individual plates, topped with cabbage wedges and sprinkled with parsley.

PREPARATION	COOKING	SERVINGS	FREEZES
15 MIN	40 MIN	6	–

RAPINI POLPETTES WITH TOMATO SAUCE

3 1/2 cups	(875 ml) tomato sauce (recipe p. 239)
1	pinch crushed red pepper flakes
1 lb	(450 g) rapini, roughly chopped
1 3/4 cups	(450 g) ricotta cheese
1/2 cup	(35 g) freshly grated Parmesan cheese
2	eggs
1	garlic clove, chopped
3/4 cup	(115 g) unbleached all-purpose flour
	Parmesan shavings, for serving
	Olive oil, for serving

In a large non-stick skillet over medium heat, heat the tomato sauce with the red pepper flakes. Keep warm.

In a pot of boiling salted water, blanch the rapini for 2 minutes. Drain. Plunge into ice water for 2 minutes. Drain again and dry on a clean tea towel.

In a food processor, purée the rapini, ricotta, Parmesan, eggs, and garlic. Transfer to a bowl. Add the flour and mix well. Season with salt and pepper.

Using a 3 tbsp (45 ml) ice cream scoop, shape the mixture into balls and place them side by side in the tomato sauce. Cover and simmer over medium-low heat for 40 minutes.

Just before serving, top with Parmesan shavings and a drizzle of olive oil. Serve as a main dish or a side.

NOTE *You can replace the rapini with two bunches of Swiss chard, stems removed and roughly chopped. You should have about 1 lb (450 g).*

PREPARATION	COOKING	SERVINGS	FREEZES
40 MIN	45 MIN	4 TO 6	–

ROASTED PEPPER AND KAMUT SALAD WITH FLANK STEAK

2	onions, chopped
2 tbsp	(30 ml) vegetable oil
4 cups	(1 L) chicken broth
3/4 cup	(150 g) whole kamut, drained and rinsed
1 lb	(450 g) beef flank steak, cut into 4 steaks
1	ball (125 g) buffalo mozzarella or 115 g feta cheese, thinly sliced
4	roasted bell peppers, mix of colours, sliced (recipe p. 225)
	Flat-leaf parsley leaves, for serving

In a pot over medium-high heat, soften the onions in 1 tbsp (15 ml) of the oil. Add the broth and kamut. Bring to a boil and let simmer for 1 hour 30 minutes or until the kamut is cooked but still al dente, stirring occasionally. Drain and mix in a little oil.

In a large non-stick skillet over medium-high heat, brown the steaks in the remaining oil for 3 to 4 minutes per side, for rare. Season with salt and pepper. Let the steaks rest on a plate for 5 minutes. On a work surface, slice the meat against the grain.

Place the kamut on plates. Tear the mozzarella overtop. Garnish with the roasted peppers and parsley. Serve with the sliced steak.

PREPARATION	COOKING	SERVINGS	FREEZES
25 MIN	1 H 40	4 TO 6	–

FRIED GREEN TOMATO BURGERS

SAUCE

1/2 cup	(125 ml) mayonnaise
1 tsp	sweet paprika
1 tsp	(5 ml) lemon juice
1	garlic clove, finely chopped
	Tabasco sauce, to taste

FRIED GREEN TOMATOES

1/2 cup	(60 g) corn flour
1 tsp	salt
1 tsp	sugar
2	eggs
1 1/2 cups	(90 g) panko breadcrumbs
2	green tomatoes, cut into 1/4-inch (5 mm) slices
	Vegetable oil, for cooking

BURGERS

4	hamburger buns, toasted
4	lettuce leaves
4	slices bacon, cooked until crispy and cut in half
1	red tomato, thinly sliced

SAUCE

In a bowl, whisk together all of the ingredients. Refrigerate until ready to use.

FRIED GREEN TOMATOES

In a shallow bowl, combine the corn flour, salt, and sugar. In another shallow bowl, beat the eggs. In a third shallow bowl, place the panko.

Dredge the green tomatoes in the flour mixture. Shake to remove any excess. Dip the tomatoes in the eggs, letting any excess drip off. Transfer them to the panko and press lightly so the panko adheres.

In a large skillet over medium-high heat, heat 1/2 inch (1 cm) of oil (topping up as needed to maintain this depth during cooking). Line a baking sheet with paper towels.

Fry half of the tomatoes at a time for 2 minutes per side or until golden brown. Let drain on the paper towels. Season lightly with salt. Let cool.

Garnish each bun with sauce, lettuce, bacon, and two slices of fried green tomato and red tomato.

Serve with baked home fries (recipe p. 39).

PREPARATION	COOKING	SERVINGS	FREEZES
30 MIN	10 MIN	4	—

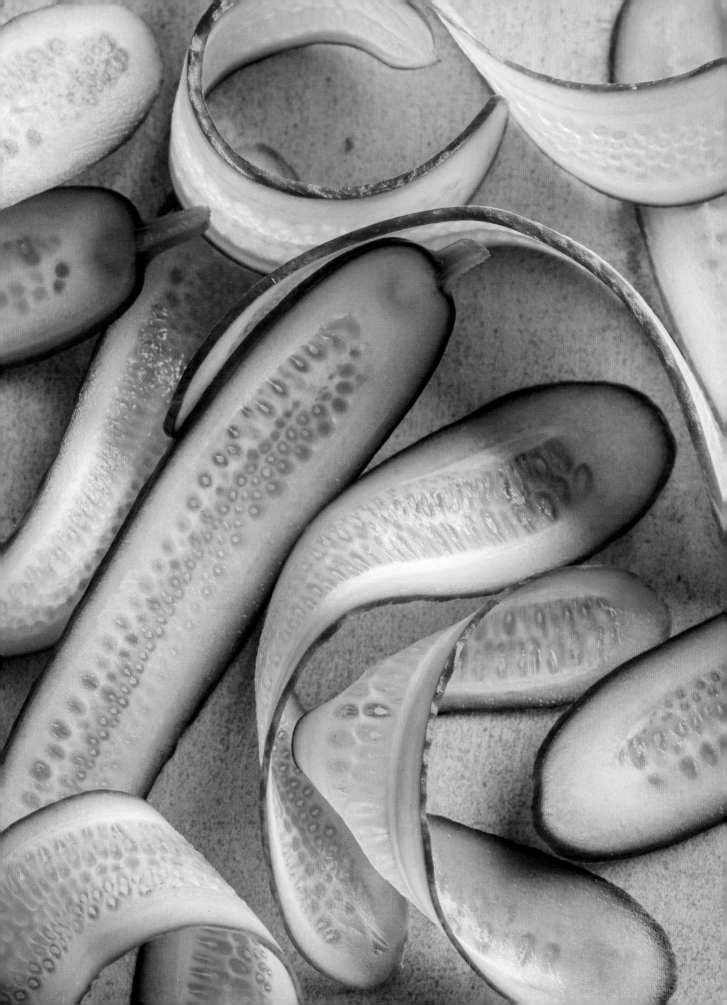

Celery Fizz

Cucumber Gin and Tonic

RAISING THE BAR

Refresh your cocktails with a ribbon of cool cucumber or a red round of beets. We'll raise a glass to these bright ideas.

Carrot, Ginger, and Rum Cocktail

Beauty and the Beet

CELERY FIZZ

1/2	celery stalk, grated
1 oz	(30 ml) gin
1/2 oz	(15 ml) lemon juice
1/2 oz	(15 ml) cane syrup
1 tsp	(5 ml) pastis
	Ice cubes
	Sparkling wine
	Celery ribbon made with a vegetable peeler, plunged in ice water for 5 minutes

In a cocktail shaker, combine the grated celery, gin, lemon juice, cane syrup, and pastis with a few ice cubes and shake vigorously. Strain into a champagne coupe. Top with sparkling wine and garnish with a celery ribbon.

PREPARATION
10 MIN

SERVINGS
1

CUCUMBER GIN AND TONIC

6	cucumber ribbons made with a vegetable peeler or mandoline
2 oz	(60 ml) gin
	Ice cubes
2	lime wedges
6 oz	(180 ml) tonic water, cold

Roll up a cucumber ribbon and pierce with a skewer. Repeat with the remaining ribbons, adding them to the same skewer.

Pour the gin into a highball glass filled with ice. Squeeze the juice from the lime wedges into the glass. Top with tonic water and garnish with the cucumber skewer to infuse the drink.

PREPARATION
10 MIN

SERVINGS
1

CARROT, GINGER, AND RUM COCKTAIL

1	carrot, sliced into rounds
1 1/2 oz	(45 ml) white rum
1 oz	(30 ml) ginger syrup (see note)
1/2 oz	(15 ml) triple sec
1/2 oz	(15 ml) lemon juice
	Ice cubes
	Carrot ribbon cut with a vegetable peeler, plunged in ice water for 5 minutes

In a blender, purée the carrot slices, rum, ginger syrup, triple sec, and lemon juice until smooth. Pass through a fine sieve.

Pour into a low-ball glass filled with ice cubes. Garnish with a carrot ribbon.

NOTE *To make a ginger syrup, bring 1/4 cup (60 ml) water, 1/4 cup (55 g) sugar, and 2 tbsp (30 ml) chopped fresh ginger to a boil. Let simmer for 5 minutes. Strain through a sieve. You will have enough syrup to make three cocktails.*

PREPARATION	SERVINGS
10 MIN	1

BEAUTY AND THE BEET

1 oz	(30 ml) vodka
1 oz	(30 ml) St-Germain Elderflower Liqueur
3/4 oz	(20 ml) lemon juice
3	thin slices beet, peeled, blanched for 1 minute, and cut in half
5	drops Angostura bitters
	Ice cubes
	Beet leaf (optional)

In a cocktail shaker, combine all of the ingredients and shake vigorously. Pour into a low-ball glass filled with ice cubes. If desired, garnish with a beet leaf.

PREPARATION	SERVINGS
10 MIN	1

VEGETABLE HORIZONS

As a kid, the only reason I knew what a fennel seed tasted like was because my father added them to the meatballs that he made every Saturday afternoon. The first time I ate grilled fennel—wow!—it was a game-changer. It was like discovering a whole new universe: both the cooking technique and the flavour were miles from the canned peas and carrots of my childhood. And full disclosure: it's only been a few years since I really started to appreciate Brussels sprouts. Once I started removing the leaves and grilling them on a baking sheet, I realized that I'd been depriving myself of a delicacy for far too long.

Depending on how they're prepared, vegetables can be a portal to other dimensions. A scalloped potato in a gratin dauphinois is no longer a humble potato. Beet carpaccio is so much more than just beets. An Indian vegetable curry takes us to warm landscapes. A bite of stuffed squash blossom conjures up a summer sunset over a table in Tuscany, or maybe just a friend's backyard in Little Italy. After all, what's exotic to one person is everyday food to someone else. That's why cooking can be so transformative.

TOMATO AND RICOTTA TARTLETS

CRUST

1	egg
1/4 cup	(60 ml) olive oil
1 tbsp	(15 ml) Dijon mustard
1/2 tsp	salt
1/4 tsp	crushed red pepper flakes
1 1/2 cups	(120 g) panko breadcrumbs

FILLING

1 cup	(260 g) ricotta cheese
2 cups	(300 g) cherry tomatoes, cut into quarters
1/4 cup	(10 g) finely chopped mixed herbs (basil, thyme, oregano, chives)
2 tbsp	(30 ml) olive oil
1/2 tsp	salt
1	pinch finely chopped garlic
1/2	lemon, zest finely grated

CRUST

With the rack in the middle position, preheat the oven to 350°F (180°C).

In a large bowl, whisk together the egg, oil, mustard, salt, and red pepper flakes. Add the breadcrumbs and mix just enough to moisten everything.

Press the mixture into six lightly oiled tartlet moulds about 4 inches (10 cm) in diameter and with removable bases. Place on a baking sheet. Bake for 20 minutes or until the crusts are golden. Let cool completely on a wire rack. Unmould and place on a serving platter.

FILLING

In a bowl, season the ricotta with salt and pepper and mix well. Divide the ricotta evenly between the tartlets.

In another bowl, gently toss the cherry tomatoes with the remaining ingredients. Season with salt and pepper. Top the tartlets with the tomato mixture.

PREPARATION	COOKING	SERVINGS	FREEZES
25 MIN	20 MIN	6	–

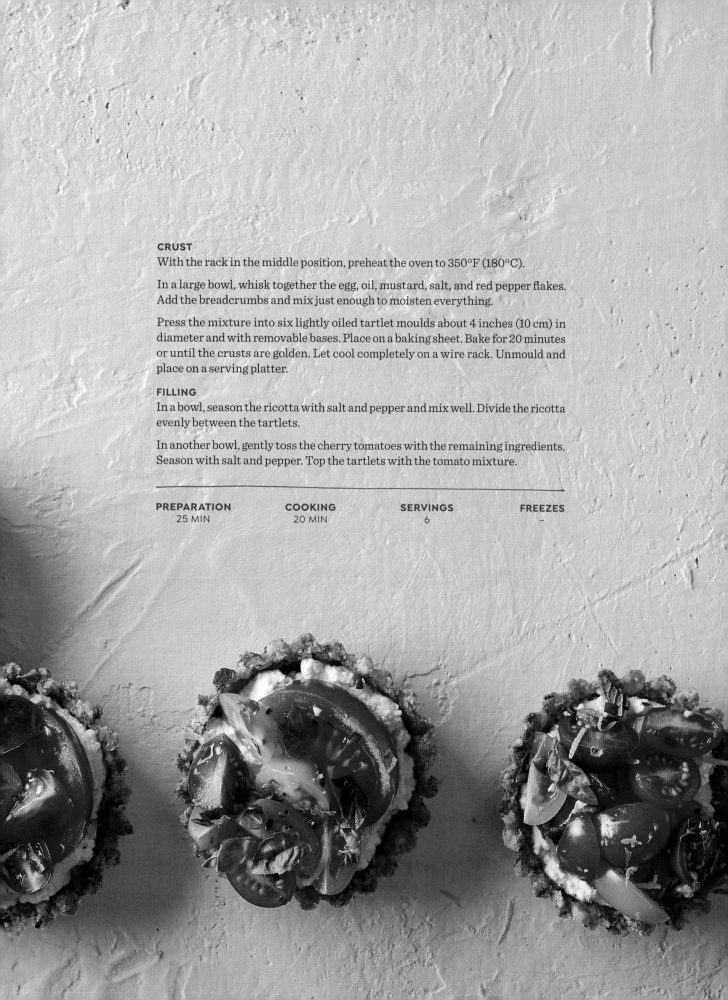

TOFU TACOS

TOFU FILLING

4	green onions, sliced
1	garlic clove, chopped
1 tbsp	(15 ml) vegetable oil
1/2	block (about 6 oz/170 g) extra-firm tofu, pressed dry and grated (see note)
1	can (19 oz/540 ml) black beans, drained and rinsed
1/2 cup	(75 g) frozen corn kernels, thawed
1/2 cup	(125 ml) vegetable broth (recipe p. 234)
1 tbsp	chili powder
1/2 tsp	ground cumin

TO SERVE

8–12	carrot juice tortillas (recipe p. 168) or wheat tortillas, warm
1 1/2 cups	(150 g) grated orange cheddar cheese
2 cups	(120 g) sliced iceberg lettuce
	Pico de gallo (recipe at right) or roasted tomato salsa (recipe p. 169)
	Sour cream, for serving

TOFU FILLING

In a pot over medium-high heat, soften the green onions and garlic in the oil. Add the tofu and cook over high heat until lightly golden. Season with salt and pepper. Add the remaining ingredients. Bring to a boil. Cover and let simmer for 15 minutes. Adjust the seasoning. Add more broth, if needed.

TO SERVE

Place the tofu filling, tortillas, cheese, lettuce, pico de gallo or roasted tomato salsa, and sour cream in the centre of the table. Everyone can garnish their own tacos.

NOTE *You can freeze the leftover tofu, whole or grated, for the next time you make tacos.*

PREPARATION	COOKING	SERVINGS	FREEZES
20 MIN	20 MIN	4	–

Roasted Tomato Salsa

PICO DE GALLO

3	Italian tomatoes, seeded and diced
1	small onion, finely chopped
1	small jalapeño pepper, deseeded and finely chopped
2 tbsp	finely chopped cilantro
2 tbsp	(30 ml) lime juice

In a bowl, combine all of the ingredients. Season with salt and pepper.

PREPARATION	MAKES
15 MIN	2 CUPS (500 ML)
COOKING	FREEZES
–	–

CARROT JUICE TORTILLAS

3 cups	(450 g) unbleached all-purpose flour
1 tsp	salt
1/4 tsp	baking powder
1 cup	(250 ml) carrot juice or cilantro juice (see note)
1/4 cup	(60 ml) vegetable oil

In a bowl, combine the flour with the salt and baking powder. Add the carrot juice and oil. Mix until well combined. Cover and let rest for 10 minutes.

Cut the dough into twelve equal pieces. On a lightly floured work surface, use a rolling pin to roll out each piece to an 8-inch (20 cm) disc.

Heat a cast iron skillet over medium-high heat. Cook one tortilla at a time for 2 minutes. Flip and continue cooking for 1 minute or until the tortilla is lightly golden. Wrap the tortillas in a clean tea towel while you continue to cook the rest.

NOTE *To make cilantro juice, blend 1 1/4 cups (50 g) of cilantro with 1 1/4 cups (310 ml) of water and a pinch of salt until smooth. Pass through a fine sieve.*

PREPARATION	COOKING	MAKES	FREEZES
25 MIN	50 MIN	12 TORTILLAS	YES

ROASTED TOMATO SALSA

1 1/2 lb	(675 g) tomatoes, cut in half and deseeded
1	jalapeño pepper or serrano chili, cut in half and deseeded
1	onion, cut into 1/2-inch (1 cm) wedges
1	garlic clove, unpeeled
1 tbsp	(15 ml) vegetable oil
1/2 cup	(15 g) cilantro leaves
2 tbsp	(30 ml) lime juice
1/4 tsp	ground cumin

With the rack in the top position, preheat the oven to broil.

On a non-stick baking sheet or a sheet lined with aluminum foil, place the tomatoes and chili cut-side down, alongside the onion and garlic. Lightly oil and season with salt and pepper.

Bake for 10 minutes or until the vegetables are blackened. Let cool. Peel the garlic clove and the tomatoes. Season with salt and pepper.

In a food processor, finely chop the onion, chili, and garlic. Add the tomatoes and cilantro. Pulse to chop. Transfer to a bowl. Add the lime juice and cumin. Adjust the seasoning. Let cool.

The salsa will keep for 1 week in an airtight container in the refrigerator.

PREPARATION	COOKING	MAKES	FREEZES
25 MIN	10 MIN	2 CUPS (500 ML)	–

Buddha Bowl

Burrito Bowl

BOWLED OVER
AN ODE TO ONE-DISH WONDERS

OUR LOVE FOR BOWLS HAS NEVER BEEN DEEPER, AND MAY EVEN BE BOTTOMLESS. BOWLS' ABILITY TO PACK IN THREE OR FOUR PORTIONS OF BRIGHT, BOLD VEGGIES, IN ADDITION TO GRAINS, LEGUMES, AND OTHER SOURCES OF PROTEIN, ALL TIED TOGETHER WITH SAUCE, MAKES THEM A TESTAMENT TO THE POWER OF PLANTS. ALL IN ONE, AND ONE FOR ALL.

Poke Bowl

BURRITO BOWL

RICE

2 cups	(500 ml) water
1 1/4 cups	(250 g) long-grain rice
1/2 tsp	salt

SAUCE

1	ripe avocado, chopped
1	small garlic clove, chopped
6 tbsp	(90 ml) water
2 tbsp	(30 ml) finely chopped cilantro
1 tbsp	(15 ml) lime juice

BOWL

2	green onions, sliced
2 tbsp	(30 ml) vegetable oil
1	can (19 oz/540 ml) black beans, drained and rinsed
1 cup	(150 g) frozen corn kernels
1	head Boston lettuce, sliced
2 tbsp	finely chopped cilantro
	Sour cream, for serving
	Pico de gallo, for serving (recipe p. 167)
	Tortilla chips (optional)

RICE

In a pot, bring the water, rice, and salt to a boil. Stir. Cover and let cook over low heat for 15 to 20 minutes. Fluff the rice with a fork. Set aside.

SAUCE

Meanwhile, in a food processor or using a handheld blender, purée all of the ingredients until smooth. Season with salt and pepper. Add water to thin out the sauce, as needed. Set aside.

BOWL

In a non-stick skillet over high heat, brown the green onions in the oil. Add the beans and cook for 2 minutes, stirring. Season with salt and pepper. Transfer to a bowl.

Add the corn to the hot skillet and cook for 2 minutes or until lightly golden. Season with salt and pepper.

Place the rice in bowls. Top with the beans, corn, lettuce, and cilantro. Drizzle with the sauce. Serve with sour cream, pico de gallo, and, if desired, tortilla chips.

NOTE *You can add cooked chicken or slices of grilled steak to this.*

PREPARATION	COOKING	SERVING	FREEZES
30 MIN	20 MIN	4	–

POKE BOWL

RICE
1 1/2 cups	(320 g) Calrose rice (sushi rice)
1 3/4 cups	(430 ml) water
1/2 tsp	salt

FISH
2 tbsp	(30 ml) soy sauce
2 tsp	(10 ml) toasted sesame oil
2 tsp	(10 ml) rice vinegar
3/4 lb	(340 g) sashimi-grade tuna or salmon, skinless and diced
2 tsp	black sesame seeds

SAUCE
1/2 cup	(125 ml) mayonnaise
2 tbsp	(30 ml) water
2 tsp	(10 ml) Sriracha sauce

BOWL
1 1/2 cups	(210 g) frozen edamame, blanched
2	Lebanese cucumbers, thinly sliced
2	carrots, finely julienned
1	avocado, diced
1/4 cup	(10 g) cilantro leaves
	Lime wedges, for serving

RICE

Rinse the rice under cold running water until the water runs clear. Drain well.

In a pot, bring the rice, water, and salt to a boil. Cover and simmer over low heat for 15 minutes or until the water has just been completely absorbed by the rice. Remove from the heat and let rest 10 minutes, covered. Remove the cover and fluff with a fork. Let cool to room temperature (see note).

FISH

In a bowl, combine the soy sauce, sesame oil, and vinegar. Add the fish and sesame seeds. Let marinate for 15 minutes.

SAUCE

In another bowl, whisk together all the ingredients until combined.

BOWL

Place the rice in bowls. Top with fish, vegetables, avocado, and cilantro. Drizzle the sauce on top. Serve with lime wedges, if desired.

NOTE *You can also use a rice cooker and cook the rice according to the manufacturer's instructions.*

PREPARATION	COOKING	MARINATING	SERVINGS	FREEZES
35 MIN	15 MIN	15 MIN	4	–

BUDDHA BOWL

SAUCE

1/3 cup	(75 ml) mayonnaise
2 tbsp	(30 ml) peanut butter
2 tbsp	(30 ml) water
1 tbsp	(15 ml) rice vinegar
1 tsp	(5 ml) sambal oelek
1 tsp	(5 ml) soy sauce

BOWL

1 tbsp	(15 ml) rice vinegar
1/2 tsp	sugar
1	pinch crushed red pepper flakes
2 cups	(170 g) sliced cabbage
1	carrot, cut into fine ribbons
1	can (19 oz/540 ml) chickpeas, drained and rinsed
1 tbsp	(15 ml) vegetable oil
1/2 lb	(225 g) green beans, trimmed and cut in half
1/2 lb	(225 g) soba noodles
1	small mango, peeled and diced
1/4 cup	(40 g) toasted salted peanuts, chopped
2 tbsp	finely chopped cilantro

SAUCE

In a small bowl, whisk all of the ingredients together until combined. Season with salt and pepper. Set aside.

BOWL

In a large bowl, mix the vinegar, sugar, and red pepper flakes together until the sugar has dissolved. Add the cabbage and carrot. Season with salt and pepper, and mix well. Let marinate for 15 minutes.

Meanwhile, in a non-stick pan over medium heat, brown the chickpeas in the oil. Season with salt and pepper. Set aside.

In a pot of boiling salted water, cook the green beans for 4 minutes or until al dente. Using a slotted spoon, remove them from the water and plunge into an ice bath to stop the cooking process. Drain. In the same pot of boiling water, cook the noodles until al dente. Drain and lightly oil.

Place the noodles in bowls. Top with cabbage, carrot, chickpeas, and green beans. Drizzle with the sauce. Garnish with mango, peanuts, and cilantro.

NOTE *You can replace the chickpeas with chicken or grilled shrimp.*

PREPARATION	MARINATING	COOKING	SERVINGS	FREEZES
30 MIN	15 MIN	12 MIN	4	–

Vegetable Chili
with Black Beans

Spinach Cornbread

VEGETABLE CHILI WITH BLACK BEANS

2	onions, chopped
3	garlic cloves, chopped
2 tbsp	(30 ml) vegetable oil
1	red bell pepper, deseeded and diced
1	jalapeño pepper, deseeded and finely chopped
3 tbsp	(25 g) chili powder
1 tbsp	sweet paprika
3/4 cup	(180 ml) vegetable or chicken broth
1	sweet potato, peeled and diced
2	cans (each 19 oz/540 ml) black beans, drained and rinsed
1	can (28 oz/796 ml) whole tomatoes, roughly crushed
1 1/2 cups	(225 g) frozen corn kernels
1/2 cup	(65 g) finely chopped toasted cashews, plus more for serving
1/2 cup	(15 g) finely chopped cilantro
	Sour cream, for serving

In a pot over medium-high heat, brown the onions and garlic in the oil. Add the bell pepper and jalapeño. Cook for 2 minutes. Add the spices and continue cooking for 30 seconds, stirring. Add the broth, sweet potato, black beans, and tomatoes. Season with salt and pepper. Bring to a boil and let simmer for 30 minutes or until the sweet potato is tender, stirring occasionally.

Add the corn and cashews. Continue cooking for 5 minutes. Add more broth if needed. Adjust the seasoning. Add the cilantro.

Serve on rice or with spinach cornbread (recipe at right) with sour cream and cashews on the side.

PREPARATION	COOKING	SERVINGS	FREEZES
20 MIN	45 MIN	6	YES

SPINACH CORNBREAD

2 cups	**(50 g) baby spinach, chopped**
2	**green onions, thinly sliced**
1 1/2 cups	**(270 g) fine cornmeal (No. 240 or No. 250)**
1 1/2 cups	**(225 g) unbleached all-purpose flour**
3 tbsp	**(40 g) sugar**
2 tsp	**baking powder**
1 tsp	**baking soda**
1/2 tsp	**salt**
3	**eggs, lightly beaten**
1 cup	**(250 ml) buttermilk**
1	**can (19 oz/540 ml) creamed corn**
1/4 cup	**(55 g) unsalted butter, melted**

With the rack in the middle position, preheat the oven to 350°F (180°C). Generously butter a cast iron or non-stick skillet about 10 inches (25 cm) in diameter.

Cover the bottom of the skillet with the spinach and green onions.

In a bowl, combine the cornmeal, flour, sugar, baking powder, baking soda, and salt. Make a well and add the eggs, buttermilk, and creamed corn. Whisk together to fully combine. Add the melted butter. Pour into the skillet over the spinach mixture.

Bake for 40 minutes or until a toothpick inserted into the centre comes out clean. Let cool on a wire rack. Serve warm or cold with soup or pulled pork.

NOTE *If you don't have buttermilk, add 1 tbsp (15 ml) of white vinegar to regular milk. Let sit for 5 minutes and then stir. You can freeze any unused buttermilk.*

PREPARATION	COOKING	SERVINGS	FREEZES
25 MIN	40 MIN	10 TO 12	YES

GREEN PEA CREPES AND WARM GREEN VEGETABLE SALAD

PEA PURÉE

2 cups	(300 g) frozen peas, thawed
1/4 cup	(60 ml) vegetable oil
1 tbsp	(15 ml) honey
1 tbsp	(15 ml) lemon juice

CREPES

2	eggs
1 cup	(150 g) unbleached all-purpose flour
1 1/4 cups	(310 ml) milk
	Melted butter, for cooking

WARM GREEN VEGETABLE SALAD

1/2 lb	(225 g) thin asparagus, trimmed and cut into 1-inch (2.5 cm) pieces
1	shallot, sliced
3 tbsp	(45 ml) vegetable oil
1 cup	(145 g) frozen shelled edamame, thawed
1	garlic clove, finely chopped
1 tsp	(5 ml) honey
2 tbsp	(30 ml) lemon juice
6 cups	(140 g) arugula

PEA PURÉE

In a blender or food processor, purée all of the ingredients until smooth. Season with salt and pepper.

CREPES

In a bowl, combine half of the pea purée with the eggs. Add the flour and 1/2 cup (125 ml) of the milk. Whisk together until the batter is smooth. Add the remaining milk gradually, whisking all the while.

Heat a non-stick skillet about 9 inches (23 cm) in diameter over medium-high heat. When the skillet is hot, brush it with melted butter.

For each crepe, pour about 3 tbsp (45 ml) of batter into the centre of the skillet. Tilt the skillet to evenly distribute the batter. When the edges begin to colour, flip the crepe over using a spatula. Continue cooking for 30 seconds until lightly coloured and then remove from the skillet.

Transfer the crepes to a baking sheet in an oven set at 200°F (95°C) while you cook the remaining crepes.

WARM GREEN VEGETABLE SALAD

In a large skillet over medium heat, soften the asparagus and shallot in 2 tbsp (30 ml) of the oil for 3 minutes. Add the edamame, garlic, and honey. Cook for 3 minutes. Add the lemon juice. Season with salt and pepper. Let cool. Add the arugula and the remaining oil just before serving.

Spread the remaining pea purée on the crepes and top with the vegetable salad. Fold the crepes in half and serve.

NOTE *The crepes are also delicious with a slice of ham, cheese, and a fried egg.*

PREPARATION	COOKING	SERVINGS	FREEZES
25 MIN	45 MIN	4	CREPES ONLY

Spring Rolls
with Peanut Sauce

SPRING ROLLS
WITH PEANUT SAUCE

PEANUT SAUCE

1/2 cup	(125 ml) water
1/4 cup	(60 ml) peanut butter
2 tbsp	brown sugar
2 tbsp	(30 ml) lime juice
1 tbsp	(15 ml) soy sauce
1 tsp	(5 ml) toasted sesame oil
1 tsp	(5 ml) sambal oelek
1	garlic clove, finely chopped

SPRING ROLLS

2 cups	(170 g) sliced red cabbage
2 tbsp	(30 ml) rice vinegar
2 tbsp	sugar
4 oz	(115 g) rice vermicelli
16	rice paper wrappers, about 8 inches (20 cm) in diameter
24	medium shrimp (31-40), cooked, chilled, and cut in half lengthwise
4	Lebanese cucumbers, julienned
3	large carrots, julienned
8	Boston lettuce leaves, cut in half
2	avocados, thinly sliced and sprinkled with lemon juice
1/2 cup	(20 g) mix of cilantro and mint leaves

PEANUT SAUCE

In a small pot, bring all of the ingredients to a boil, whisking frequently. Let simmer for 2 minutes or until the sauce thickens. Transfer to a bowl. Cover and let cool. Stir before serving.

SPRING ROLLS

In a bowl, combine the cabbage with the vinegar and sugar. Let marinate for 15 minutes. Drain.

Plunge the rice vermicelli into a pot of boiling water. Remove from the heat and let sit for 3 minutes or until tender. Drain and rinse under cold running water. Drain well.

Dip one rice paper wrapper at a time into a large shallow bowl filled with hot water for a few seconds or until softened. Remove from the water. Dry on a clean towel and place on a clean, flat work surface, such as a counter or plastic cutting board (avoid using a wooden board as the rice paper can stick to it). Place another rice paper wrapper overlapping half of the first one.

Place three shrimp halves on the first third of the wrapper. Add the cabbage, cucumber, and carrot, letting them overhang the wrapper slightly. Place 1/4 cup (60 ml) of rice vermicelli on top of the vegetables. Top with two pieces of lettuce leaf and a few slices of avocado. Tightly roll for one and a half turns. Add another three shrimp halves and a few cilantro and mint leaves. Finish rolling up tightly to enclose the filling.

Cover the rolls with a clean damp towel while you form the others. Cut each roll in three. Serve immediately with the peanut sauce.

PREPARATION	COOKING	MARINATING	MAKES	FREEZES
45 MIN	8 MIN	15 MIN	8 ROLLS	–

Greek Burgers

GREEK BURGERS

TZATZIKI

1/2 cup	(100 g) grated English cucumber
1/2 cup	(125 ml) plain Greek yogurt
2 tbsp	finely chopped mint
1	small garlic clove, finely chopped

GRILLED VEGETABLES

1 tbsp	(15 ml) olive oil
1	yellow bell pepper, deseeded and cut into quarters, or 1 roasted bell pepper (recipe p. 225)
1	red onion, cut into 1/2-inch (1 cm) slices

PATTIES

1 lb	(450 g) ground lamb or veal
1/4 cup	(35 g) oil-packed sun-dried tomatoes, chopped
1/4 cup	(10 g) finely chopped flat-leaf parsley

SPINACH

1	small garlic clove, thinly sliced
1 tbsp	(15 ml) olive oil
6 cups	(140 g) baby spinach

HAMBURGERS

4	hamburger buns
4	slices tomato
2 oz	(55 g) sliced feta cheese

TZATZIKI

Drain the cucumber in a sieve, pressing down to remove as much liquid as possible.

In a bowl, combine the cucumber and the remaining ingredients. Season with salt and pepper. Set aside.

GRILLED VEGETABLES

Place a grill wok on the barbeque. Preheat the grill to medium-high. Oil the grate beside the wok to cook the patties.

Oil the bell pepper (if using raw) and onion. Season with salt and pepper. Grill the onion in the wok for a few minutes. Add the bell pepper, skin-side down. Grill for 8 to 10 minutes or until the bell pepper skin is blackened and the onion cooked. Place the bell pepper in an airtight container. Let cool to room temperature. Peel the skin off the pepper and keep warm with the onion.

PATTIES

In a bowl, combine all of the ingredients. Season with salt and pepper. With lightly oiled hands or using a hamburger press, shape the meat into four thin patties. Season with salt and pepper.

Grill the patties for 4 to 5 minutes per side or until fully cooked.

SPINACH

In a large non-stick skillet over medium heat, soften the garlic in the oil. Add the spinach and continue to cook for 1 minute or until wilted. Season with salt and pepper. Drain, if necessary. Keep warm.

HAMBURGERS

Toast the hamburger buns. Spread the inside of the buns with tzatziki. Place the spinach on the bottom halves of the buns. Top with the patties, bell pepper, onions, tomato, and feta. Place the top halves on the buns.

NOTE *If you don't have a barbeque, you can use a hot cast iron grill pan to cook the vegetables and patties.*

PREPARATION	COOKING	SERVINGS	FREEZES
40 MIN	25 MIN	4	–

LEEK TART

1	egg
1 tbsp	(15 ml) water
4 oz	(115 g) fresh goat cheese
2 tbsp	(30 ml) 35% cream
1/2 lb	(225 g) frozen puff pastry, thawed
2 cups	(500 ml) buttered leeks (recipe p. 230)
2 tbsp	finely chopped flat-leaf parsley

With the rack in the middle position, preheat the oven to 400°F (200°C). Line a baking sheet with a silicone mat or parchment paper.

In a small bowl, combine the egg with the water, whisking with a fork until smooth. Set aside.

In another bowl, mix the cheese with the cream, whisking with a fork until combined. Set aside.

On a lightly floured work surface, roll out the puff pastry to a 10-inch (25 cm) square. Trim four strips, each 1/2-inch (1 cm) wide, from each side of the puff pastry. Place the square on the baking sheet. Using a pastry brush, brush the edges of the dough with some of the egg mixture. Place the strips of dough along the edges of the crust and press lightly to adhere. Brush the edges of the dough with the egg mixture.

Spread a layer of the cheese mixture within the borders of the pastry and top with a thick layer of leeks.

Bake for 35 minutes or until the dough is golden brown. Let cool for 10 minutes. Sprinkle with the parsley and cut into squares.

Delicious hot or cold, as an appetizer or as a light lunch with a salad.

PREPARATION	COOKING	SERVINGS	FREEZES
25 MIN	35 MIN	12	–

BUTTERNUT SQUASH GNOCCHI WITH SAGE BROWN BUTTER

GNOCCHI

1 1/4 cups	(310 ml) butternut squash purée (recipe p. 229)
1/2 cup	(115 g) butter
1/4 cup	(60 ml) water
1 1/2 tsp	salt
1 1/2 cups	(225 g) unbleached all-purpose flour
3	eggs
1/4 cup	(20 g) finely grated Mimolette, Pacific Rock, or aged orange cheddar cheese

SAUCE

6 tbsp	(85 g) butter
5	sage leaves
1/4 tsp	crushed red pepper flakes
	Shavings of Mimolette, Pacific Rock, or aged orange cheddar cheese, for serving

GNOCCHI

In a pot, bring the squash purée, butter, water, and salt to a boil. Remove from the heat. Add the flour all at once and mix vigorously with a wooden spoon until the dough becomes smooth and pulls away from the sides of the pot.

Place the pot back over medium heat and cook the dough, stirring constantly, for 2 minutes, or until the dough dries slightly. Place in a bowl or the bowl of a stand mixer.

Using a wooden spoon or the paddle attachment, add the eggs, one at a time, mixing thoroughly between each addition, until the dough is smooth and combined. Add the cheese. Transfer to a piping bag fitted with a 1/2-inch (1 cm) plain tip.

Using a knife, cut the gnocchi about 1-inch (2.5 cm) long as you let them fall into a pot of boiling salted water. Cook one-quarter of them at time. Once they begin to float, let them simmer for 1 minute. Remove them with a slotted spoon and place on a lightly oiled baking sheet. Continue with the remaining dough. The gnocchi can be frozen at this stage, if desired.

SAUCE

In a large non-stick skillet over medium heat, cook the butter until it browns. Add the sage, red pepper flakes, and gnocchi. Mix well to coat the gnocchi.

Garnish with the cheese shavings and serve as an appetizer or side dish. Delicious with grilled pork, chicken cutlets, or roasted lamb.

PREPARATION	COOKING	SERVINGS	FREEZES
30 MIN	30 MIN	4	YES

RATATOUILLE TIAN

1 cup	(250 ml) tomato sauce (recipe p. 239)
2	garlic cloves, finely chopped
1/4 cup	(60 ml) torn basil leaves
2	zucchini (1 yellow, 1 green) sliced into 1/4-inch (5 mm) rounds
2	small Italian eggplants or 1 Japanese eggplant, cut into 1/4-inch (5 mm) rounds
1/3 cup	(75 ml) olive oil
4	Italian tomatoes, cut into 1/4-inch (5 mm) rounds

With the rack in the middle position, preheat the oven to 375°F (190°C).

In a glass or ceramic dish 9 inches (23 cm) in diameter, combine the tomato sauce, garlic, and basil. Set aside.

In a bowl, combine the zucchini, eggplants, and oil. Season generously with salt and pepper.

Alternate the vegetables and tomatoes to make a spiral on top of the tomato sauce. Cover with aluminum foil. Place on a baking sheet.

Bake for 1 hour. Remove from the oven. Remove the foil and baste the vegetables with the cooking juices.

Return to the oven, uncovered, for 30 minutes or until the vegetables are tender and the liquid has almost evaporated.

Serve hot or at room temperature. Delicious as an appetizer or with grilled meat.

PREPARATION	COOKING	SERVINGS	FREEZES
25 MIN	1 H 30	6	–

ONION AND CHEESE BREAD

3 1/2 cups	(525 g) unbleached all-purpose flour
2 tsp	salt
1/2 tsp	instant yeast
1 3/4 cups	(430 ml) cold water
2 cups	(200 g) grated aged orange cheddar cheese
1/2 cup	(125 ml) caramelized onions (recipe p. 238)

In a large bowl, combine the flour, salt, and yeast. Add the water. Using a fork, mix until the water is well distributed but the dough is still rough. Add the cheese and onions. Cover with plastic wrap and let rise for 8 to 12 hours at room temperature.

Using your hands and keeping the dough in the bowl, punch down the dough by folding it over on itself six times.

Butter a 10- x 4-inch (25 x 10 cm) loaf pan with a 6-cup (1.5 L) capacity. Line with a piece of parchment paper, letting it hang over the sides. Transfer the dough to the loaf pan. Cover with lightly oiled plastic wrap and let rise for 1 hour at room temperature or until the dough is slightly higher than the top of the loaf pan.

With the rack in the middle position, preheat the oven to 400°F (200°C).

Bake for 1 hour. Let cool on a wire rack for 15 minutes. Unmould and let cool completely.

PREPARATION	RISING	COOKING	MAKES	FREEZES
20 MIN	9 H	1 H	1 LOAF	YES

ASPARAGUS AND GOAT CHEESE TART

CRUST
1/4 cup	(35 g) toasted hazelnuts
1/2 cup	(75 g) unbleached all-purpose flour
1/2 cup	(75 g) whole wheat flour
2 tsp	thyme leaves
1/8 tsp	salt
6 tbsp	(85 g) unsalted butter, cold and cut into cubes
2 tbsp	(30 ml) 35% cream

FILLING
4 oz	(115 g) fresh goat cheese
3 tbsp	(45 ml) 35% cream
1 lb	(450 g) mix of blanched vegetables (wild asparagus or thin asparagus cut in half lengthwise and sprouting broccoli) (see note)
2 tbsp	(30 ml) olive oil
1 tbsp	(15 ml) white wine vinegar
	Chopped, toasted hazelnuts, for serving

CRUST

In a food processor, chop the hazelnuts with both flours. Add the thyme and salt. Mix to combine. Add the butter and pulse until the butter is pea-sized. Add the cream and pulse until the dough comes together.

Place the dough in a tart mould 9 inches (23 cm) in diameter and with a removable bottom. Press the dough evenly on the bottom and sides of the mould. Refrigerate for 30 minutes.

With the rack in the middle position, preheat the oven to 400°F (200°C).

Using a fork, prick the bottom of the tart shell. Bake for 20 minutes or until the crust is golden. Let cool completely on a wire rack.

FILLING

In a bowl, combine the goat cheese and cream. Season with salt and pepper. Spread evenly across the bottom of the cooled tart shell.

In another bowl, combine the vegetables with the oil and vinegar. Season with salt and pepper. Arrange the vegetables on top of the cheese. Sprinkle with hazelnuts and serve.

NOTE *Wild asparagus is not technically asparagus but is marketed under that name. You can find it in select grocery stores in the spring. Sprouting broccoli is also sold under the names broccolini. In this recipe, it can be replaced with rapini or broccoli.*

PREPARATION	COOLING	COOKING	SERVINGS	FREEZES
30 MIN	1 H	25 MIN	6	–

Squash and Roasted Vegetable Lasagne

SQUASH AND ROASTED VEGETABLE LASAGNE

ROASTED VEGETABLES

1	large eggplant, cut into 1/2-inch (1 cm) slices
1/4 cup	(60 ml) olive oil
2	bell peppers, mix of colours, deseeded and cut into 1/4-inch (5 mm) rounds
1	zucchini, cut into 1/4-inch (5 mm) rounds

LASAGNE

12 to 16	lasagne noodles (see note)
1 tbsp	(15 ml) butter
13 cups	(300 g) baby spinach
4 cups	(1 L) tomato sauce (recipe p. 239)
3 cups	(300 g) grated mozzarella cheese
2 cups	(500 ml) butternut squash purée (recipe p. 229)
1/2 cup	(35 g) freshly grated Parmesan cheese
5 oz	(140 g) thinly sliced provolone cheese

ROASTED VEGETABLES

With two racks in the middle positions, preheat the oven to 425°F (220°C). Line two baking sheets with parchment paper.

On one of the baking sheets, combine the eggplant with 3 tbsp (45 ml) of the oil. Season with salt and pepper. On the other baking sheet, combine the bell peppers and zucchini with the remaining oil. Season with salt and pepper. Lay the vegetables out in a single layer, if possible. Bake the two sheets for 20 to 25 minutes or until the vegetables are roasted. Set aside a few vegetables for the top of the lasagne.

Turn down the oven to 375°F (190°C).

LASAGNE

Meanwhile, in a pot of boiling salted water, cook the noodles until al dente. Drain and oil lightly.

In the same pot over medium-high heat, melt the butter. Add the spinach and cook for 1 to 2 minutes or until just wilted. Drain slightly. Set aside a few leaves for the top of the lasagne.

In a 13- x 9-inch (33 x 23 cm) baking dish, spread 1 cup (250 ml) of the tomato sauce and cover with a layer of pasta. Add a layer of eggplant and spinach. Add 1 cup (250 ml) of the tomato sauce and half of the mozzarella. Add a layer of pasta and cover with squash purée. Sprinkle with half of the Parmesan and a layer of pasta. Add the zucchini and bell peppers. Add 1 cup (250 ml) of the tomato sauce and sprinkle with the remaining mozzarella. Top with a final layer of pasta and the remaining tomato sauce, provolone, the reserved vegetables, and spinach. Sprinkle with the remaining Parmesan. Place on a baking sheet.

Bake for 45 minutes, and then brown under the broiler, if desired. Let rest for 15 minutes before serving.

NOTE *The amount of pasta needed may vary depending on the brand used and the size of the baking dish.*

PREPARATION	COOKING	SERVING	FREEZES
35 MIN	1 H 10	8	YES

POACHED PATTY PAN SQUASH WITH CLAMS

2 cups	(500 ml) chicken broth
6	fingerling potatoes, cut into 1/2-inch (1 cm) slices
2	garlic cloves, chopped
3 tbsp	(40 g) butter
1 tbsp	(15 ml) lemon juice
1 lb	(450 g) patty pan squash or zucchini, cut into 1/2-inch (1 cm) slices or Ronde de Nice squash, cut into 1/2-inch (1 cm) wedges
3	radishes, thinly sliced
1	shallot, chopped
1/2	jalapeño pepper, deseeded and chopped
36	clams, scrubbed
1	lemon, zest finely grated

In a large pot or skillet over high heat, bring the broth, potatoes, and garlic to a boil. Cover and let simmer gently for 10 minutes or until the potatoes are al dente. Uncover and let the liquid reduce by half.

Add the butter and lemon juice, and then the vegetables (including the jalapeño). Cover and continue cooking for 3 minutes or until the vegetables are al dente. Remove the vegetables using a slotted spoon. Keep warm in a bowl. Season the broth to taste.

In the same pot over high heat, add the clams to the broth. Cover and let simmer gently for 4 minutes or until the clams open. Discard any clams that remain closed.

Transfer the vegetables and clams to shallow bowls. Sprinkle with the lemon zest.

PREPARATION	COOKING	SERVING	FREEZES
20 MIN	30 MIN	4	—

CAULIFLOWER PURÉE WITH SCALLOPS AND ROASTED ROOT VEGETABLES

ROOT VEGETABLES (SEE NOTE)

2	small yellow beets, peeled and cut into 1/2-inch (1 cm) slices
1	large carrot, peeled and cut into 1/2-inch (1 cm) slices
1	purple carrot, peeled and cut into 1/2-inch (1 cm) slices
2 tbsp	(30 ml) vegetable oil

CAULIFLOWER PURÉE

1	small Russet potato, peeled and cubed
1/2	cauliflower, chopped
2 tbsp	(30 ml) butter

SCALLOPS

1 lb	(450 g) large scallops (10–12), trimmed and patted dry
1 tbsp	(15 ml) vegetable oil
1 tbsp	(15 ml) butter
1/4 cup	(45 g) pomegranate seeds
2 tbsp	roughly chopped chives

ROOT VEGETABLES

With the rack in the middle position, preheat the oven to 425°F (220°C).

In an 11- x 8-inch (28 x 20 cm) glass baking dish, combine the vegetables with the oil. Season with salt and pepper. Cover with aluminum foil. Bake for 15 minutes. Turn the vegetables and continue cooking, uncovered, for 20 minutes or until the vegetables are tender and golden. Set aside.

CAULIFLOWER PURÉE

Meanwhile, in a pot of boiling salted water, cook the potato for 5 minutes. Add the cauliflower and cook until both vegetables are tender. Drain.

Transfer to a food processor. Add the butter and purée until smooth. Using a spatula, scrape down the sides of the processor bowl occasionally. Season with salt.

SCALLOPS

In a large skillet over medium-high heat, brown the scallops in the oil and butter. Season with salt and pepper.

Place the purée in the centre of the plates. Top with the vegetables and scallops. Sprinkle with the pomegranate seeds and chives.

NOTE *This recipe is also delicious with other root vegetables, such as sweet potatoes, parsnip, salsify, turnip, celeriac, etc.*

PREPARATION	COOKING	SERVINGS	FREEZES
50 MIN	40 MIN	4	–

Spinach Falafel
Sandwiches

SPINACH FALAFEL
SANDWICHES

FALAFEL

1 cup	(205 g) dried chickpeas, drained and rinsed (see note)
6 cups	(140 g) baby spinach, or a mix of spinach and kale
1/2 cup	(23 g) cilantro leaves
1	small onion, chopped
2	garlic cloves, chopped
2 tsp	ground coriander
1 1/2 tsp	ground cumin
1/2 tsp	baking powder
1/2 tsp	salt
3 tbsp	(25 g) chickpea flour (or 30 g unbleached all-purpose flour)
	Canola oil, for frying

BEET

1	large red beet, peeled and julienned
1 tbsp	(15 ml) lemon juice

SANDWICH

4 to 6	naan breads, toasted
1 cup	(250 ml) store-bought hummus or carrot and cashew dip (recipe p. 24)
2 cups	(50 g) sliced Boston lettuce leaves
	Lemon wedges, for serving

FALAFEL

In a large bowl, cover the chickpeas with cold water and let soak for 12 hours or overnight at room temperature. Add water as needed to keep them covered. Rinse and drain.

In a food processor, finely chop the spinach. Add the cilantro, onion, garlic, and soaked chickpeas. Reduce to a fine paste. Add the ground spices, baking powder, and salt, and mix until well combined. Incorporate the flour.

Using a 3-tbsp (45 ml) ice cream scoop, shape the mixture into balls and place them on a large plate. Using your hands, flatten the balls into patties.

In a large skillet, heat 1 inch (2.5 cm) of oil to 350°F (180°C). Line a baking sheet with two layers of paper towel.

Fry a few falafel at a time for about 3 to 4 minutes, turning halfway through cooking, or until they are golden and crispy. Drain on the paper towel. Season with salt.

BEET

In a pot of boiling salted water, blanch the beet for 1 minute. Drain and cool under cold running water. Drain well.

In a bowl, combine the beet and lemon juice. Season with salt and pepper.

SANDWICH

Spread the naan breads with hummus. Top with lettuce, falafel, and beet. Serve with a lemon wedge.

NOTE *In this recipe, you can't use canned chickpeas since they are already cooked and will make the mixture too soft and difficult to work with.*

PREPARATION	SOAKING	COOKING	SERVINGS	FREEZES
55 MIN	12 H	15 MIN	4 TO 6	FALAFEL ONLY

FAMILY-STYLE SPANAKOPITA

1	onion, chopped
3 tbsp	(45 ml) olive oil
16 cups	(310 g) baby spinach
1 cup	(30 g) finely chopped flat-leaf parsley
1 cup	(25 g) finely chopped dill
1 2/3 cups	(200 g) crumbled feta cheese
2	eggs, beaten
3	garlic cloves, chopped
1 tsp	(5 ml) dried oregano
1	lemon, zest finely grated
9	sheets phyllo pastry
1/2 cup	(115 g) unsalted butter, melted

With the rack in the middle position, preheat the oven to 350°F (180°C).

In a large non-stick skillet over medium-high heat, soften the onion in the oil.

Add the spinach and herbs. Cook, stirring, until the spinach is wilted. Drain the spinach well, pressing on it with the back of a wooden spoon to remove most of the liquid. Place in a bowl and let cool.

Add the feta, eggs, garlic, oregano, and lemon zest to the spinach. Season with pepper and mix well.

On a work surface, layer four sheets of phyllo on top of one another, brushing each one with the melted butter. Line an 8-inch (20 cm) square baking dish with the phyllo. Top with the spinach mixture and fold in the edges of the phyllo over top.

Cut the remaining five sheets of phyllo in half lengthwise to make ten rectangles. Brush the rectangles one at a time with the melted butter. Place one buttered rectangle on the dough in the baking dish. Crumple the rest with your hands to resemble roses and place them one at a time on top.

Bake for 45 minutes or until the spanakopita is golden. Let cool for 20 minutes before cutting.

PREPARATION	COOKING	SERVINGS	FREEZES
35 MIN	55 MIN	9	–

Pea-Stuffed Pasta

PEA-STUFFED PASTA

PASTA

3	egg yolks
2	whole eggs
1 tbsp	(15 ml) olive oil
1 3/4 cups	(265 g) unbleached all-purpose flour
1/2 tsp	salt

FILLING

2 cups	(300 g) frozen peas
3	green onions, sliced
1 tbsp	(15 ml) butter

PASTA

In a bowl, whisk together the yolks, whole eggs, and oil.

In a food processor, combine the flour and salt. Add the egg mixture. Process for 30 seconds. The dough will not form a ball, but will be clumpy. If it does form a ball, add 1 tbsp of flour at a time until it starts to clump. If it is too dry, add water, 1 tbsp (15 ml) at a time, as needed.

Place the dough on a work surface and press the pieces together. Knead for 2 minutes or until the dough is smooth and comes together. Wrap in plastic wrap and let rest for 30 minutes at room temperature.

FILLING

Meanwhile, in a pot of boiling salted water, blanch the peas and green onions for 2 minutes. Drain. Transfer to a food processor. Add the butter and purée until smooth. Using a spatula, scrape the sides of the processor bowl occasionally. Season with salt and pepper. Transfer to a piping bag fitted with a 1/2-inch (1 cm) plain tip. Set aside.

TO SHAPE

On a floured work surface, divide the dough into four pieces and shape into rectangles. Using a pasta roller, roll out one rectangle at a time, adding just enough flour to keep it from sticking. Start at the thickest setting and continue passing the dough through until you reach setting 5 or 6 or the dough is translucent. The dough should be about 5 1/2 inches (14 cm) wide. Keep the other pieces of pasta covered while you work.

Place a sheet of pasta dough on a lightly floured work surface. Cut the sheet in half lengthwise to make two long strips. Cut each strip into rectangles 3 inches (7.5 ml) long.

Pipe about 1 to 2 tsp (5 to 10 ml) of filling in the centre of each rectangle. Brush the edges of the pasta with a bit of water. Roll the pasta over the filling into a tube and pinch the edges to seal. It should look like a wrapped caramel. Transfer to a lightly floured baking sheet. It can be frozen at this stage, if desired.

In a pot of boiling salted water, cook half of the pasta at a time until tender, about 4 minutes. Drain.

Serve the pasta immediately, tossed with melted butter and a mix of chopped herbs (basil, parsley, chives) or tarragon sauce (recipe p. 219).

PREPARATION	RESTING	COOKING	SERVINGS	FREEZES
1 H 20	30 MIN	10 MIN	6	YES

PEA-STUFFED PASTA WITH TARRAGON SAUCE

TARRAGON SAUCE

1	shallot, chopped
3 tbsp	(40 g) butter
4 cups	(1 L) chicken broth
3	sprigs tarragon
3	slices lemon, deseeded
1/4 cup	(60 ml) 35% cream

GARNISH

1 cup	(150 g) frozen peas
1/4 lb	(115 g) sugar snap peas, trimmed
1 tsp	finely chopped fresh tarragon
1	recipe pea-stuffed pasta (recipe p. 216)

TARRAGON SAUCE

In a skillet over high heat, soften the shallot in the butter. Add the broth, tarragon, and lemon. Bring to a boil and let reduce by half, about 15 minutes. Remove the lemon and tarragon. Over medium heat, add the cream. Season with salt and pepper.

GARNISH

Meanwhile, in a pot of boiling salted water, blanch the peas and sugar snap peas for 2 minutes. Remove them with a slotted spoon and rinse under cold running water. Drain. If desired, separate the sugar snap peas in half lengthwise.

In the same pot of boiling salted water, cook half of the pasta at a time until tender, about 4 minutes. Drain.

Add the pasta to the sauce. Warm through for 2 minutes, stirring to coat the pasta with the sauce. Adjust the seasoning if needed.

Transfer the pasta to plates and top with the peas and sugar snap peas. Sprinkle with the tarragon. Serve as an appetizer.

PREPARATION	COOKING	SERVINGS	FREEZES
15 MIN	30 MIN	6	–

GROWING A LEGACY

While it may have taken me years to come around to enjoying more diverse types of vegetables, my daughters have grown up experiencing the fuller spectrum of what nature provides. Like me, they know what it's like to be greeted by their grandmother on their return from school, with a little paring knife for cutting veggies and a dip at the ready. In many ways, our path through food can reflect our path through life—it evolves as we do. I've certainly changed over time, my tastes have changed, and the way I eat has changed. I like to think that I've given my children an appreciation for vegetables and for the gardens those vegetables took root in.

Roasted Bell Peppers

Pickled Celery

Sweet Pickles

PICKLED CELERY

3	large celery stalks, cut into 1–inch (2.5 cm) pieces (or 6 small stalks cut into large matchsticks)
1 cup	(250 ml) water
1/2 cup	(125 ml) white vinegar
1/4 cup	(55 g) sugar
1/2 tsp	salt
1/2 tsp	coriander seeds

In a glass jar with a 2-cup (500 ml) capacity, place the celery pieces.

In a small pot, bring the rest of the ingredients to a boil. Pour the marinade over the celery to cover. Close the jar and let cool for 30 minutes. Refrigerate and let cool completely, about 3 hours.

Delicious with grilled meats or as an antipasto. The pickled celery will keep for 1 month in the refrigerator.

PREPARATION	COOKING	COOLING	MAKES	FREEZES
10 MIN	5 MIN	3 H 30	2 CUPS (500 ML)	–

ROASTED BELL PEPPERS

| 6 | bell peppers, mix of colours, cut in half and deseeded |
| 2 tbsp | (30 ml) vegetable oil |

With the rack in the middle position, preheat the oven to 450°F (230°C).

On a non-stick baking sheet or a sheet lined with parchment paper, place the peppers cut-side down. Drizzle with oil. Bake for 30 minutes or until tender and golden. Place the peppers in an airtight container and let cool for 20 minutes. Remove the skin.

Perfect in roasted pepper and kamut salad (recipe p. 153) or Greek burgers (recipe p. 188), or as an antipasto.

The roasted bell peppers will keep for 2 weeks in an airtight container in the refrigerator.

PREPARATION	COOKING	COOLING	MAKES	FREEZES
20 MIN	30 MIN	20 MIN	3 CUPS (750 ML)	YES

SWEET PICKLES

5 1/2 lb	(2.5 kg) unpeeled garden cucumbers, or pickling cucumbers (see note)
8	onions, peeled (2 lb/900 g)
2	bell peppers (1 yellow, 1 green), deseeded and cut into thin strips
1/2 cup	(125 g) coarse pickling salt
5 cups	(1 kg) sugar
4 cups	(1 L) white vinegar
2 tbsp	yellow mustard seeds
1 1/2 tsp	ground turmeric
1/2 tsp	cloves
1/2 tsp	celery seeds

On a work surface, cut off and discard one end of each cucumber. Using a mandoline, slice the cucumbers 1/8 inch (3 mm) thick. Discard the other ends of the cucumbers as well, as they can make the pickles soft if used. You will get 16 cups (4 L) of cucumber. Place in a large bowl. Repeat with the onions. Add to the cucumbers and mix well with the bell peppers and pickling salt. Let marinate for 3 hours at room temperature. Rinse and drain well.

In the bottom of a canning pot, place the jar holder and add the jars. Cover with hot water. Place over medium heat and bring to a simmer. Turn down the heat to its lowest setting and leave the jars in the warm water while you prepare the pickles. Remove from the water just before filling the jars.

Place the lids (discs) in a small pot and cover with water. Bring to a simmer, turn off the heat, and keep the lids in the hot, but not boiling, water until ready to use. This will soften the rubber rings.

In a large pot, bring the sugar, vinegar, and spices to a boil. Add the drained vegetables. Bring to a boil again, stirring occasionally. Remove from the heat.

Transfer the vegetables and syrup to the hot jars, leaving 1/2 inch (1 cm) of space at the top of each jar. Remove any air bubbles with a non-metallic utensil, such as a heatproof spatula, and wipe the rim of the jar with a clean towel.

Centre the lids (discs) on the jars and screw the rings down until the point of resistance, then tighten another eighth-turn, without forcing them.

Place the jars upright on the canning rack in the pot of hot water. Make sure the water is at least 1 inch (2.5 cm) higher than the tops of the jars. Cover the pot. Bring to a boil over high heat. Counting from the moment the water starts to boil, process for 15 minutes to sterilize.

Remove the jars from the water and place them upright on a folded towel. Let cool for 24 hours without tightening the lids. You should hear the lids seal as they cool. You can check the seal after 24 hours by pressing on the lid. If there is no movement, it means it has sealed properly. If they are not sealed, you can keep them in the refrigerator and eat them within a few weeks. The sealed jars will keep for 1 year in a cool, dark place.

NOTE *Pickling cucumbers are in season during the summer, usually August and September.*

PREPARATION	MARINATING	COOKING	MAKES	FREEZES
30 MIN	3 H	20 MIN	EIGHT 2-CUP (500 ML) JARS	–

BUTTERNUT SQUASH PURÉE

| 1 | large butternut squash (about 3 1/2 lb/1.6 kg) |
| | Vegetable broth, as needed |

With the rack in the middle position, preheat the oven to 375°F (190°C). Line a baking sheet with a silicone mat or parchment paper.

On a work surface, cut the squash in half lengthwise and remove and discard the seeds. Place the squash skin-side down on the baking sheet. Bake for 50 minutes or until fork-tender. Let cool.

Using a spoon, remove the flesh and place it in a food processor. Purée until smooth. Add vegetable broth if needed, to thin the purée. Season with salt and pepper.

You can use the purée in the squash and roasted vegetable lasagne (recipe p. 202) or butternut squash gnocchi with sage brown butter (recipe p. 192), or alongside grilled poultry. The purée will keep for 1 week in an airtight container in the refrigerator.

PREPARATION	COOKING	MAKES	FREEZES
15 MIN	50 MIN	4 CUPS (1 L)	YES

BUTTERED LEEKS

2.2 lb	(1 kg) finely sliced leeks (white and tender green parts only) (about 6 leeks)
1/4 cup	(55 g) butter
1/4 cup	(60 ml) chicken broth

In a large pot over medium-high heat, soften the leeks in the butter for 5 minutes. Add the broth and let simmer over medium heat for 15 minutes until the leeks are tender and the broth is almost completely evaporated. Season with salt and pepper. Let cool.

Use in leek tart (recipe p. 191) or leek soup (recipe p. 48), or freeze in 1-cup (250 ml) containers to add to soups. Buttered leeks will keep for 1 week in an airtight container in the refrigerator.

PREPARATION	COOKING	MAKES	FREEZES
15 MIN	20 MIN	4 CUPS (1 L)	YES

CRUSHED RED PEPPER FLAKES

Bird's eye chilies

With the rack in the middle position, preheat the oven to 175°F (80°C). Line a baking sheet with parchment paper.

Arrange the chilies on the baking sheet so they aren't touching each other. Dry in the oven for 3 to 4 hours or until they are dry and crumble easily. Let cool completely.

Remove the stems. In a food processor, or using a mortar and pestle, crush the chilies. Be careful, as the spice will be in the air as well as on your hands. The pepper flakes will keep for 1 year in an airtight container at room temperature.

NOTE *Larger chilies (like Fresno, cherry, cayenne, and Portuguese) require more drying time, up to 8 hours. Let them cool in the oven once the heat has been turned off until you are ready to crush them. They can also be dried in a food dehydrator in accordance with the manufacturer's instructions.*

PREPARATION	COOKING	MAKES	FREEZES
5 MIN	3 TO 4 H	VARIES DEPENDING ON THE NUMBER OF CHILIES	–

VEGETABLE BROTH

16 cups	(4 L) water
2	large carrots, unpeeled, cut into 1/2-inch (1 cm) slices
2	celery stalks, cut into 1/2-inch (1 cm) slices
2	garlic cloves, peeled
1	onion, unpeeled and roughly chopped
1	leek, cut into 1/2-inch (1 cm) slices
1/2 oz	(15 g) dried porcini mushrooms
2	sprigs thyme
2	sprigs flat-leaf parsley
1	bay leaf
1 tsp	salt

In a large pot, place all of the ingredients. Bring to a boil and let simmer for 1 hour over medium heat or until the broth has reduced by half. Pass through a sieve. Discard the vegetables. You will have about 8 cups (2 L) of broth.

Delicious in soups or sauces, or used to cook certain vegetables.

PREPARATION	COOKING	MAKES	FREEZES
15 MIN	1 H 15	8 CUPS (2 L)	YES

VEGETABLE DEMI-GLACE

1/2 lb	(225 g) white mushrooms, sliced
1	onion, unpeeled, roughly chopped
2	garlic cloves, unpeeled, crushed
3 tbsp	(45 ml) vegetable oil
2 tbsp	(30 ml) tomato paste
2 tbsp	(30 ml) white wine
2 cups	(500 ml) vegetable broth (recipe p. 234)
1 tsp	onion powder
1 tsp	garlic powder
1 tsp	dried parsley
1 tsp	salt
2 tbsp	nutritional yeast (see note)

With the rack in the middle position, preheat the oven to 400°F (200°C).

On a non-stick baking sheet, combine the vegetables with the oil. Bake for 20 to 25 minutes or until the vegetables are golden, stirring twice. Remove from the oven. Add the tomato paste and mix well. Return to the oven and bake for 3 to 5 minutes or until the tomato paste has caramelized.

Place the roasted vegetables in a pot. Deglaze the baking sheet with the wine and scrape the bottom to loosen any caramelized bits. Pour into the pot. Add the broth, spices, and salt. Bring to a boil and let simmer until the broth has reduced by half and the demi-glace coats the back of a spoon, about 20 minutes. Add the yeast, stirring to dissolve. Pass through a sieve. Adjust the seasoning.

Use the demi-glace in the recipe of your choice, such as onion soup or sauces. It will keep for 2 weeks in an airtight container in the refrigerator.

NOTE *Nutritional yeast boosts the flavour of this demi-glace. You can find it in select grocery stores or natural food stores. You can sprinkle it on dishes as a garnish. Not to be confused with baker's yeast, which is granulated while nutritional yeast is flakey.*

PREPARATION	COOKING	MAKES	FREEZES
20 MIN	45 MIN	1 CUP (250 ML)	YES

CARAMELIZED ONIONS

5 lb   (2.3 kg) onions, sliced
2 tbsp   (30 ml) vegetable oil

With the rack in the middle position, preheat the oven to 425°F (220°C).

On a non-stick baking sheet, combine the onions with the oil. Season with salt and pepper.

Bake for 1 hour 45 minutes, stirring every 10 minutes, until the onions are well browned. Let the sheet cool on a wire rack. Use in onion and cheese bread (recipe p. 196), onion soup, a sandwich, or freeze in 1/2 cup (125 ml) portions. The caramelized onions will keep for 1 week in an airtight container in the refrigerator.

PREPARATION
30 MIN

COOKING
1 H 45

MAKES
2 CUPS (500 ML)

FREEZES
YES

TOMATO SAUCE

1	onion, finely chopped
2	garlic cloves, finely chopped
2 tbsp	(30 ml) olive oil
2	cans (each 28 oz/796 ml) whole Italian tomatoes, crushed
2 tbsp	finely chopped basil leaves

In a pot over medium heat, brown the onion and garlic in the oil. Add the tomatoes and let simmer for 30 minutes. Add the basil. Season with salt and pepper.

PREPARATION 10 MIN	**MAKES** 6 CUPS (1.5 L)
COOKING 40 MIN	**FREEZES** YES

ROASTED GARLIC

| 4 | heads garlic |
| 2 tbsp | (30 ml) vegetable oil |

With the rack in the middle position, preheat the oven to 350°F (180°C).

Slice the top off the heads of garlic so that each clove is exposed. Drizzle the oil over the garlic. Season with salt and pepper. Wrap in aluminum foil.

Bake for 45 minutes or until tender. Let cool. Press on the base of the garlic to squeeze out the cloves.

Delicious in mashed potatoes, soups, vinaigrettes, or softened butter. The roasted garlic will keep for 3 weeks in an airtight container in the refrigerator.

NOTE *You can save energy by making these when you have something else in the oven. At 400°F (200°C), the cooking time will be 30 minutes.*

PREPARATION	COOKING	MAKES	FREEZES
5 MIN	45 MIN	3/4 CUP (180 ML)	YES

WASTE NOT, WANT NOT

squash

Celeriac

onions

leek

cabbage

cucumber

sweet potato

turnip

broccoli

carrot

cauliflower

vegetables for PURÉE

Discarded leaves, peels, wilted bits, and leftovers; most unused parts of plant-based foods can be transformed into something more, like broths, soups, or purées. We like to take a simple, straightforward approach to reusing these: just store unused portions and scraps in pre-labelled plastic bags in a designated spot in your freezer. When a bag gets full, it's time to turn the contents into a useful and wholesome recipe. This cuts down not only on food costs, but also on food waste.

INSTRUCTIONS FOR MAKING PURÉE: *Place 4 cups (1 L) of cubed potatoes and 2 cups (125 mL) of cubed vegetables in a pot. Cover with cold water. Season with salt. Bring to a boil and let simmer until the vegetables are tender, about 25 minutes. Drain. Return the vegetables to the pot. Using a potato masher, mash them with 1/4 cup (55 g) of butter. Then, using an electric mixer, whip with 1/2 cup (125 ml) of milk until smooth. Season with salt and pepper.*

cauliflower
squash
carrots
celeriac
sweet potato
broccoli
corn on the cob
parsnip
beans
Swiss chard
asparagus

green onions
celery
leek
mushrooms
tomatoes
bell peppers
garlic
herbs
carrot
fennel
onion
shallots

vegetables for SOUP

vegetables for BROTH

INSTRUCTIONS FOR MAKING SOUP: In a pot, brown 1 chopped onion and 1 chopped garlic clove in 2 tbsp (30 ml) of olive oil. Add 4 cups (1 L) of vegetables, 1 can of beans (drained and rinsed), and 5 cups (1.25 L) of chicken or vegetable broth. Let simmer until the vegetables are tender. Transfer to a blender and blend until smooth. Season with salt and pepper.

INSTRUCTIONS FOR MAKING BROTH: In a large pot, place 6 cups (1.5 L) of whole or large roughly chopped vegetables with 16 cups (4 L) of water. Bring to a boil and let simmer over medium heat for 1 hour or until the broth is reduced by half. Pass through a sieve. Discard the vegetables and reserve the broth. You will have 8 cups (2 L) of vegetable broth.

Corn on the cob

KEEPING THINGS FRESH

Once they've been picked, vegetables don't all have the same shelf life. These storage tips will help you keep your vegetables in the best possible condition so you can use them while they're in tip-top shape.

herbs

tomatoes

unripe avocado

squash

garlic

onions

potatoes

shallots

sweet potato

bean sprouts

arugula

ripe avocado

Cauliflower

mushrooms   broccoli

chilies

bell peppers

green onions

artichoke

celery

beets *

*When you buy them, separate root vegetables from their leaves. The roots will last for several weeks; the leaves, for 2–3 days.

watercress

beans

bok choy

radicchio

endives

head of lettuce

radishes*

Jerusalem artichokes

asparagus

eggplant

zucchini

loose leaf lettuce

spinach

Brussels sprouts

baby potatoes

leek

cucumber

carrots

celeriac

cabbage

1-2 days

3-4 days

5-7 days

2-4 weeks

Thanks

First and foremost, I'm dedicating this cookbook to farmers. Thank you for growing such delicious vegetables, for being stewards of the earth, for enriching our culture, and for standing tall in the face of globalization. A special thanks to the grocers and purveyors who believe in and encourage local agriculture. Your entrepreneurial strength has the power to change our society for the better.

Writing a book is kind of like cooking—it's possible to do it alone, but it's even better when people you admire are involved. I want to thank everyone who brought their passion to this project. You're a truly sensitive, smart, and stimulating team. Many thanks to the talented group at Appetite by Random House, for your confidence and shared enthusiasm for this book.

When I married a nutritionist, vegetables were included in the contract. So an extra special thanks to my wife and Editorial Director, Brigitte, for spearheading this book and setting a wonderful example for our girls and our company.

Last but not least, I would like to express my deepest gratitude to my readers who continually inspire me. Your needs and eating habits are changing, and I am listening to you as we grow together. Thanks for always expecting nothing but the best.

INDEX

INDEX BY VEGETABLE

TOMATO

Eggplant Parmesan, 116

Fried Green Tomato Burgers, 155

Pico de Gallo, 167

Ratatouille Tian, 194

Roasted Tomatoes in Oil and Balsamic
Vinegar, 14

Roasted Tomato Salsa, 169

Tomato and Ricotta Tartlets, 164

Tomato Juice, 60

Tomato Sauce, 239

Vegetable Chili with Black Beans, 178

Vegetable Pizzas with Parmesan, 130

Wedge Salad, 90

TUSCAN KALE

Tuscan Kale Pesto, 77

ZUCCHINI

Ratatouille Tian, 194

Spiralized Zucchini Fries, 44

Squash and Roasted Vegetable Lasagne, 202

Vegetable Pizzas with Parmesan, 130

Zucchini with Parmesan, 17

WITHOUT VEGETABLES

Béarnaise Sauce, 86

Béchamel Sauce, 87

Chili and Lime Salt, 22

Hollandaise Sauce, 87

Pistachio Dukka, 23

Pizza Dough, 131

Sesame Salt, 22

Traditional Vinaigrette, 86

INDEX BY TYPE OF RECIPE